CONTENTS

KU-585-230

Written and researched by
Tony Kelly: updated by Pamela Scales

The contents of this guidebook are believed correct at the time of printing.
Attractions and establishments may open, close or change and Thomas Cook
Holdings Ltd cannot accept responsibility for errors or omissions, or for the
consequences of any reliance on the information provided. Descriptions and
assessments are based on the author's views and experience at the time of
writing and these do not necessarily represent those of Thomas Cook Holdings.
We would be grateful to be told of any changes or updates; please notify
them to the Commissioning Editor at the address below.

Thomas Cook Publishing, Thomas Cook Holdings Ltd, PO Box 227,
Peterborough PE3 8XX, United Kingdom.
E-mail: books@thomascook.com

Opposite: Fishing village, Binibeca Vell

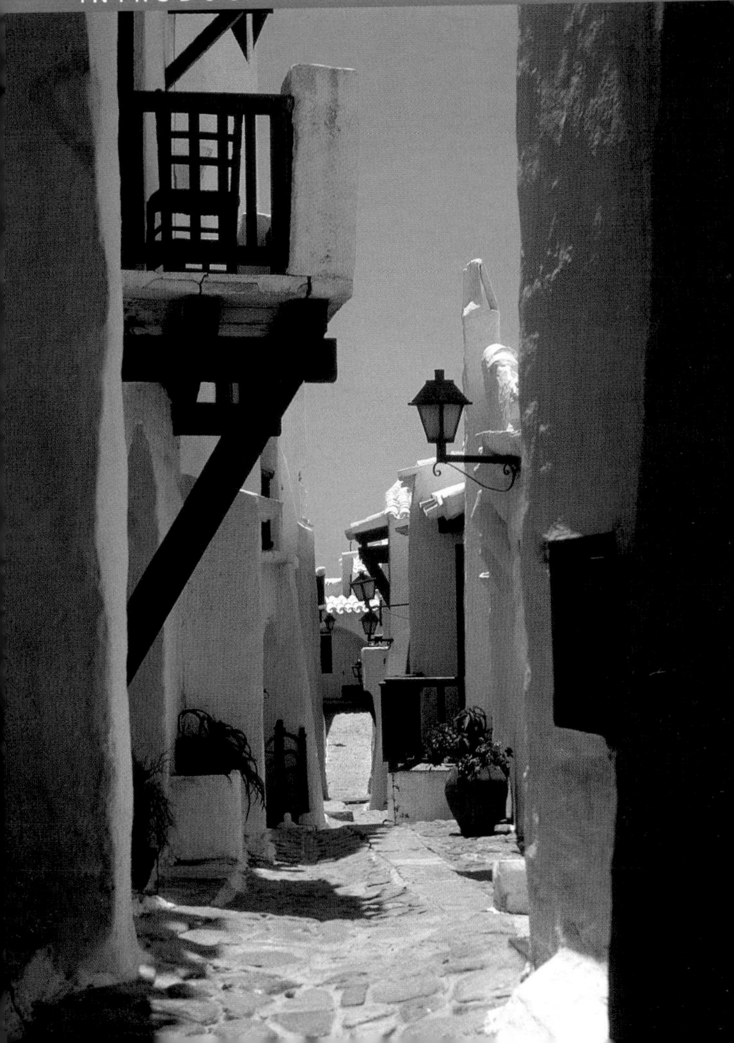

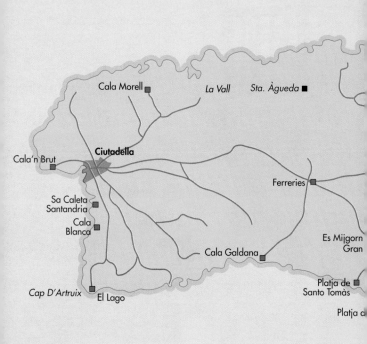

Cala Morell

La Vall   *Sta. Àgueda* ■

Ciutadella

Cala'n Brut

Ferreries

Sa Caleta
Santandria
Cala
Blanca

Es Mijgorn
Gran

Cala Galdana

Platja de
Santo Tomàs

Cap D'Artruix   El Lago

Platja c

MEDITERRANEAN SEA

0   5   10 km

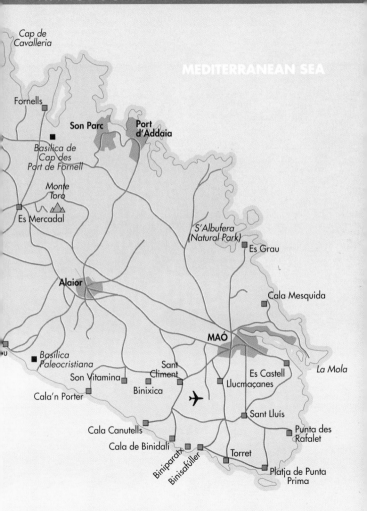

Cap de
Cavalleria

MEDITERRANEAN SEA

Fornells

Son Parc   Port
d'Addaia

Basílica de
Cap des
Port de Fornell

Monte
Toro

Es Mercadal

S'Albufera
(Natural Park)

Es Grau

Alaior

Cala Mesquida

MAÓ

La Mola

Basílica
Paleocristiana

Son Vitamina   Sant
Climent   Es Castell
Llucmaçanes

Cala'n Porter   Binixica

Sant Lluís

Cala Canutells   Punta des
Rafalet

Cala de Binidali

Biniparatx   Torret

Binisafúller

Platja de Punta
Prima

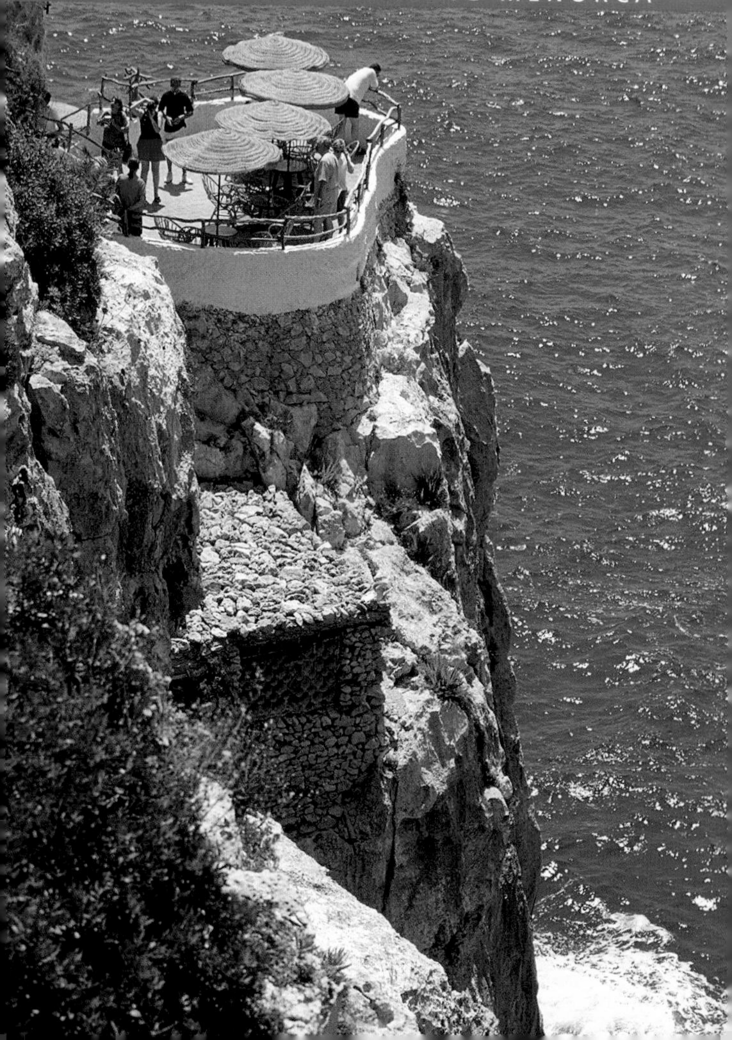

Getting to know Menorca

Azure skies, endless sunshine and beaches of pale gold sand washed by a turquoise sea – Menorca has all the ingredients for a relaxing holiday. Its beaches are some of the finest in Europe, from fun-packed family resorts to secret pine-fringed coves that can only be reached on foot. Its calm, clear waters are perfect for swimming and snorkelling, or for learning to windsurf and sail. The peaceful countryside of rolling hills, meadows and dry-stone walls forms a gentle backdrop to the rocky coast, and the main towns at either end of the island are an intriguing contrast of history, culture and style.

SERENE AND GENTLE ISLE

Each of Spain's Balearic Islands has its own personality. Menorca – also spelt Minorca – has often lived in the shadow of its larger neighbour, Mallorca, but it is quite happy to be known as the quieter and more relaxed of the two. It has little of the hectic nightlife of Ibiza, though there is plenty of fun to be had after dark for those who seek it. Menorca's character is different – serene, courteous, gentle, just right for a family holiday.

THE BALEARICS

Menorca is the second largest of the Balearic islands, a group of islands off the east coast of Spain in the western Mediterranean. Mallorca is just 21 miles (34km) away and the nearest city on the Spanish mainland is Barcelona, 140 miles (225km) to the north west. Menorca lies about half-way between Marseilles, in the south of France, and Algeria, on the north coast of Africa.

Cova d'En Xoroi, near Cala'n Porter

Above all, Menorca is a place to unwind, to eat the freshest seafood while listening to the sound of the waves, to walk across a herb-scented headland to find that hidden beach, to watch the sun set over the sea and enjoy the smiles on the faces of your children, enchanted by the magic of it all.

A LITTLE HISTORY

Menorca's history goes back a long way – to the Talaiotic period of around 2000BC. Not much is known of the island's early inhabitants, but they left behind a wealth of prehistoric monuments, from watch-towers to burial caves. Later invaders left their mark too – the Romans introduced Christianity to the island and established a city at Maó, the Arabs introduced horses, still a Menorcan passion, and the Catalan conquest of 1287 opened the way for Menorca to become a part of modern Spain.

THE BRITISH CONNECTION

Menorca was ruled by the British for 70 years during the 18th century and the British influence on the island remains strong. It was the British who introduced Friesian cattle and helped to develop the dairy industry, which is still so important today. The first British governor built a road across the island, moved the capital to Maó, planted orchards and introduced new breeds of sheep and poultry. Several words in the Menorcan dialect derive from English – such as *mervils* (marbles) and *boinder* (which means a bow window, as seen in the old Georgian houses in Maó).

THE TWO CITIES

Maó and Ciutadella may be only 30 miles (48km) apart but they face in different directions, as if they were deliberately turning their backs on one another. Maó, the modern capital, is a bustling city of businesses and government offices, with an old town of stylish shopping streets and one of the world's great harbours. Ciutadella, at the other end of the island, is much more traditional, with a Gothic cathedral surrounded by the palaces of the Catalan nobility, who refused to leave the city when the capital was moved to Maó. As a result, Ciutadella is much the most Spanish place on Menorca.

Castell de Sant Nicolau, Ciutadella

Settling in

MONEY MATTERS

In line with the majority of EU member states, Spain entered the single currency on 1 January 2002, with the peseta accepted as dual currency up to 28 February. Euro (€) note denominations are 500, 200, 100, 50, 20, 10 and 5. Coins are 1 and 2 euros and 1, 2, 5, 10, 20 and 50 céntimos. A euro equals 166.385 pesetas.Banks open Mon–Fri 0830–1415.

HEALTH AND HYGIENE

Health hazards: people who are not used to the sun burn easily – and children are especially vulnerable. It is a good idea to cover up with a strong sunblock, wear a hat and keep out of the midday sun by taking a siesta in the shade. In a hot climate you also need to drink a lot more water and soft drinks. The tap water is safe to drink but can be very salty. Mineral water is widely available and cheap. Swimming is generally safe but keep a look out for the safety flags on the larger beaches and never go in when the red flag is flying. It is not a good idea to swim after drinking alcohol.

Pharmacies: in towns and main resorts. There is also a chemist open 24 hours by rota, which is posted on all pharmacy doors.

SHOPS AND SERVICES

Shops: the Spanish custom of taking a siesta during the afternoon means that most shops are open 0930–1330 and 1730–2030 Monday to Friday, and 0930–1330 on Saturday. In the resorts, some open all day and at weekends; the big supermarkets on the outskirts of Maó and Ciutadella open 0900–2100 Monday to Saturday and 0900–1300 on Sunday.

Post: stamps can be bought at post offices, tobacconists' shops and at souvenir shops which also sell postcards.

WHAT TO DO IN AN EMERGENCY
The general emergency telephone number is **112**. You can call an ambulance on **061** and the police on **091**.

PHONING ABROAD?

To call an overseas number, dial **00** followed by the country code (UK = **44**), then the area code (minus the initial 0) and then the number you want.

Phones: phone kiosks are everywhere, with instructions in several languages. Phonecards are available in post offices and shops for 6 euros or 12 euros. You can also use your credit card in most public phones. Some bars and kiosks have metered phones where you can make your call first and pay for it afterwards. Cheap rate is from 2200 to 0800 on Sundays and official fiestas. Local calls are very cheap. Remember to dial the local code for the Balearic Islands (971) before each number (as listed in this book).

CRIME AND EMERGENCIES

Crime: there is no more crime on Menorca than anywhere else in Europe but you should always take sensible precautions. Don't leave money or valuables unattended on the beach or by the pool, and if you have a hire car you should lock your possessions out of sight in the boot.

Medical: if you have medical insurance or are willing to pay, you can contact the private Salus health clinic. The lines are open 24 hours a day and the staff speak English. The freephone number is 900 605050.

Dental: treatment is not usually covered by insurance, but in an emergency contact Salus health clinic (*tel: as above*).

Consular services: if you lose your passport or get into trouble with the police, contact the UK vice-consulate (*tel: 971 363373*) in Es Castell.

MOORISH NAMES

After the Christian reconquest, many Moors continued to inhabit towns throughout the region until they were officially expelled in 1609. Inland towns still bear traces of their Moorish legacy in their ruined castles, their architecture or even in their names; many have the prefix 'Bini', which means 'son of' in Arabic.

Getting around

Buses: From the bus station in Maó buses run 6 times daily along the main road from Maó to Ciutadella and there are also bus services from Maó to Es Castell, Sant Lluís, Binibeca, Es Canutells, Cala'n Porter, Son Bou, Cala Galdana, Arenal d'en Castell, Son Parc and Fornells, and from Ciutadella to Cala Galdana, Cala'n Bosch, Sa Caleta and Cala'n Forcat.

Taxis: These are available in all of the main resorts. The taxis are not metered, so you should check the fare in advance. Drivers keep a list of fares for the most common routes and you can ask to see this. A tip is always welcome!

Hiring a car: There are car hire offices in all the main resorts – the biggest local company is Betacar. To hire a car you need your driving licence and you should keep this on you at all times, along with the hire documents and a copy of your passport.

RULES OF THE ROAD
The speed limits are 55mph (90kmh) on the main highway, 30mph (50kmh) in towns and 20mph (30kmh) on country roads, unless indicated otherwise. These are strictly enforced, as are the drink-driving laws (it is illegal to drink alcohol and drive). Children must sit in the back and young children need a special seat – tell the hire firm if you need one (some firms charge extra for this). Seatbelts must be worn at all times. Some country roads are very narrow and you should always take care, especially on blind bends.

PETROL
There are several petrol stations around Maó and Ciutadella and along the main road between the two, but few on the rest of the island so it is worth keeping the tank topped up. Most petrol stations are open 0700–2100 and a few are open 24 hrs. Most of the others have self-service machines outside these hours where you can pay for your petrol in advance using Spanish banknotes. All hire cars take the unleaded petrol known as Eurosuper, or *sin plomo*.

The language

Since 1983 the official language of Menorca has been Catalan, but Spanish is also widely spoken and many people speak English and German, especially in the resorts. The change from Spanish to Catalan in recent years has been very gradual, and street signs could be in either Spanish or Catalan. The capital, Maó, is known as Mahón in Spanish; Ciutadella is known as Ciudadela.

The people of Menorca speak Menorquín (the dialect of Catalan spoken on Menorca) rather than Spanish, and they are proud of the difference between the two languages. However, they understand Spanish and don't expect tourists to be good at Menorquín.

yes	*sí*
no	*no*
please	*por favor*
thank you	*(muchas) gracias*
hello	*hola*
goodbye	*adiós*
good day	*buenos días*
good afternoon	*buenas tardes*
good night	*buenas noches*
excuse me	*perdón*
help!	*¡socorro!*
today	*hoy*
tomorrow	*mañana*
yesterday	*ayer*
how much?	*¿cuanto?*
expensive	*caro*
open	*abierto*
closed	*cerrado*
bank	*el banco*
exchange bureau	*la oficina de cambio*
post office	*correos*
change money	*cambiar dinero*
bank card	*la tarjeta del banco*

The best of Menorca

BEACHES

Take a ride on a pedalo, swim in the sea or just lie on the beach soaking up the sun. Here are some of Menorca's best beaches, with facilities for all the family:

- South coast – Binibeca and Punta Prima (*page 36*), Cala'n Porter (*page 44*), Son Bou (*page 50*), Santo Tomàs (*page 54*) and Cala Galdana (*page 58*).
- West coast – Sa Caleta/Cala Santandría and Cala'n Bosch/Son Xoriguer (*page 64*).
- North coast – Arenal d'en Castell and Son Parc (*page 80*), and Playa de Fornells/Cala Tirant (*page 76*).

SECLUDED COVES

Menorca has some 216 km of coastline with many small coves as well as the larger beaches. Most of these smaller coves can be reached either on foot or along farm tracks, after paying a small entrance fee when crossing private land. They are often pine-fringed, with beautiful clear water, although they have no facilities. Nevertheless, they are very popular with the local people and are extremely busy at the weekends. Try Arenal de Son Saura and Cala'n Turqueta, both reached across farmland south of Ciutadella (*page 98*), or Cala Pregonda, on the north coast near Fornells (*page 74*) – or take a boat trip from Cala Galdana (*page 56*) or Cala'n Bosch (*page 62*) to visit the many unspoiled beaches along the south coast.

AND MORE...

- Wander the back streets of Maó (*page 16*) and Ciutadella (*page 98*), browsing in small, specialist shops among the hidden alleyways.
- Visit Maó's market (*page 21*) to taste some Mahón cheese, take a boat tour around Maó harbour (*page 30*), then look into the Xoriguer distillery on the waterfront to sample the local *pomada* (gin with lemon).
- Visit Monte Toro (*page 89*), Menorca's highest point, with sea views on all sides.

Ferreries

- Try *caldereta de langosta* (lobster casserole) beside the harbour at Fornells (*page 77*).

- Have lunch in Ciutadella harbour (*page 103*) beneath the old city walls.

- Go to the trotting races (*page 118*) in Maó and Ciutadella at weekends – and have a flutter.

- Learn about Menorca's history – complete with sound effects – at Fort Marlborough (*page 30*) near Es Castell.

- See the whitewashed 'fishing village' at Binibeca Vell (*page 36*).

- Seek out some of Menorca's ancient monuments, such as the Naveta d'es Tudons burial chamber near Ciutadella (*page 100*).

- Watch the sun go down on the west coast (*pages 63 and 67*), with Mallorca silhouetted on the horizon … then watch the moon come up from the Xoroi caves in Cala'n Porter (*page 47*).

Beneath the city walls

Maó – stately Georgian capital

Founded in Roman times and rebuilt after the Catalan
conquest, the city of Maó – also known as Mahón –
reached its heyday when the first British governor, Sir
Richard Kane, moved the capital here from Ciutadella
in 1722. You can still feel the British influence today,
in streets like Carrer Isabel II, whose fine Georgian
houses are adorned with sash windows.

Maó (pronounced 'Ma-oh') is a city for strolling, especially along the pedestrian shopping streets which tumble down the hill from the main square, Plaça de S'Esplanada, to the port. Wander down any of the side streets and you come across hidden alleys, stylish shops or an unexpected glimpse of an ancient archway, the only surviving section of the old city walls.

Plaça de S'Esplanada is the city's meeting place, where children play and old men sit beneath the trees while the bustling life of a modern capital goes on all around them – the best place to watch it all happening is from one of the cafés lining the square.

DID YOU KNOW?
Maó, or Mahón as it is frequently called, gave mayonnaise to the world. The word was invented by the amorous French duke of Richelieu who used it as an aphrodisiac – *mahonesa* translates as 'a girl from Mahón'!

THINGS TO SEE AND DO

Local museums *
Ateneu is Maó's natural history museum (*Carrer de Cifuentes 25; tel: 971 360553; open Mon–Sat 1000–1400 & 1600–2000*), with magnificent cabinets of stuffed seabirds, spiny crabs and lobsters, shells, seaweed and fossils. Keen historians should visit the **Collecció Hernández Mora** (*Claustre del Carme; tel: 971 350597; open Mon–Sat 1000–1300; closed Sun*), a fascinating collection of island maps bequeathed to the city by a local author.

Museu de Menorca ***
This museum, in the cloisters of the former Franciscan convent, contains finds from the many Bronze Age sites that have been discovered on Menorca in recent years. *Plaça d'es Monestir. Open Apr–Sept Tues–Sat 1000–1400 & 1700–2000, Sun 1000–1400, closed Mon; Oct–Mar Tues–Sat 1000–1300 & 1600–1800, Sun 1000–1400, closed Mon.*

Teatro Principal ***
There are a variety of concerts throughout the season advertised in the local press. *Costa d'en Deia 46, Mahon. Tel: 971 355776.*

Museu de Menorca

Carrer de Ciutadella

Carrer de S'Arraval

Town

Igle
Santa

Hann
(Costa d

Carrer Rovellada de Dalt

Av José M Quadrado

P

7

8

Municipal
Theatre

Co

Ateneu

6

P

De Ses Moreres (Dr. Orfila)

Plaça de
s'Esplanada

2

Carrer de Sant Josep

Parc d'es
Freginal

P

Bus
Station

Carrer de M Lluïsa Serra

Carrer Josep Ansel Clavé

Carrer es Còs

Carrer de Pedro Maria Cardona

C. sa Sínia Costabella

PORT DE MAÓ

eral / C. Moret

Library

Collecció
Hernández Mora

Police
Station

Carrer de Bellavista

Carrer del Carme

n Deiá

Camí des Castell

R I Cajal

Carrer de Gràcia

Carrer de la Infanta

Carrer de Sant Manuel

Santa Maria *

The highlight of Maó's biggest church is its Swiss organ, with more than 3,000 pipes. Organ concerts are given here between July and September, at 1100 every morning except Sundays.

EXCURSION

Albufera d'es Grau **

This beautiful Natural Park, centred around a massive lagoon about half-way between Arenal d'en Castell and Maó, is a paradise for walkers, bird-watchers and nature-lovers. Look out for such species as the tree frog, the ruin lizard, the aquatic terrapin, the booted eagle and the brightly coloured bee-eater. The long, sandy beach at Es Grau is ideal for children, with clear, shallow water and boat excursions to the Illa d'en Colom, Menorca's largest offshore island, named after a notorious pirate.

 It is almost impossible to find a parking space in the city centre – your best bet is to arrive by bus, or failing that, drive down to the harbour where there is usually a little more space; or use the underground car parks below Plaça de S'Esplanada and Plaça Miranda in the centre of town.

RESTAURANTS AND BARS (see map on pages 18–19)

Most of Maó's best restaurants are down by the waterfront on the road around the harbour. Here is a selection of eating places in the city centre.

 American Bar £ ❶ A pleasant place to watch the world go by. The square outside is a popular meeting place. *Plaça Reial. Tel: 971 361822. Open 0600–2200.*

Casa Sexto ££ ❷ Charming, family-run restaurant and *tapas* bar with a wide choice of meat, fish and shellfish dishes. Also try the home-made Galician wine, served in traditional style, in white pottery cups. *Carrer Vassallo 2. Tel: 971 368407. Open 1100–1600 & 2000–midnight.*

SHOPPING

Catolica A good bookshop for maps and books on Menorca, and copies of the local English-language magazine *Roqueta*. *Carrer Hannover 14. Open 0930–1330 & 1700–2000. Closed Sat pm and Sun.*

Local produce – try Vallès bakery at Carrer Hannover 19 for cakes, chocolates and giant *ensaimadas* (light, fluffy buns dusted with icing sugar), and the long-established El Turronero confectioners at Carrer Nou 22–26, for such delicious treats as nougat, sugared almonds, and toffee, lemon and meringue-flavoured ice-creams.

Market Maó's covered market is beautifully situated in the cloisters of an old Carmelite church. This is a good place to pick up everything you need for an afternoon picnic on the beach, such as bread, fruit, almonds, Mahón cheese, cured ham and several varieties of Menorcan pork sausages. The fish market is in a separate building down the road. *Open Mon–Sat, mornings only.*

The Old Town The streets between Plaça de S'Esplanada and the market are where you will find Maó's most stylish boutiques. For good leather bags and shoes, look out for Jaime Mascaro and Patricia in Carrer Ses Moreres; Marisa and Mark's in Carrer Hannover; Milady in Carrer Nou; and Pons Quintana and Torres in S'Arravaleta. Other shops include Mango, also in S'Arravaleta, for fashions, and a branch of the Body Shop in Carrer Nou..

SYP Large supermarket with its major outlets on Maó's industrial estate (signposted POIMA) and on the main road from Maó to Sant Lluis. *Open Mon–Sat 0900–2200, Sun 0900–1400.*

Mirador Café £ ❸ This friendly café, overlooking the harbour, attracts a young crowd. Bar snacks include delicious filled rolls and unusual salads. *Plaça Espanya 2. Open Mon–Sat 1000–0100. Closed Sun.*

Ses Palmeras £ ❹ Popular with locals and visitors alike, centrally situated in Placa Colon. *6, Mahon. Tel: 971 364717. Open Mon–Fri 0700–2200, Sat 0700–1500. Closed Sun.*

San José ££ ❺ The specialities at this British farmhouse restaurant include crispy Yorkshire duck and a steamed steak-and-mushroom pudding, available at 24 hours' notice. *Booking advised. Just outside Maó on the road to Fornells. Tel: 971 351759. Open Mon–Sat from 1900, Sun from 1300.*

Sa Parada £ ❻ The *tapas* here are good and cheap, and the setting beside the main square makes it a great place for people-watching. *Plaça de S'Esplanada 64. Tel: 971 365213. Open Mon–Sat 0800–2200. Closed Sun.*

Pilar £££ ❼ More like eating in a private home than a restaurant – top-quality Mediterranean cooking in a back-street house with a garden terrace. Expensive, but special. *Booking advised. Carrer des Forn 61. Tel: 971 366817. Open Thurs–Sat 1330–1500, Mon–Sat 2030–2330.*

La Tropical ££ ❽ There are only a few outdoor tables on a busy street, but this typical Spanish restaurant serves some of the best and freshest food in town. Try the 'menu from the market', which changes daily. *Carrer La Lluna 36. Tel: 971 360556. Open 1300–1600 & 1930–2330.*

NIGHTLIFE

Maó's main nightlife district is down on the waterfront at Moll de Ponent (*see page 31*), but there are a few fashionable nightspots in the town centre as well:

Si The only centrally located disco in town, popular with locals and tourists alike. *Carrer Verge de Gràcia 16. Tel: 971 361362. Open 2330–0300.*

Maó's tranquil back streets

Café Blues Trendy basement bar, playing mostly jazz and blues. *Carrer Santiago Ramon i Cajal 3. Open Tues–Sun from 1900. Closed Mon.*

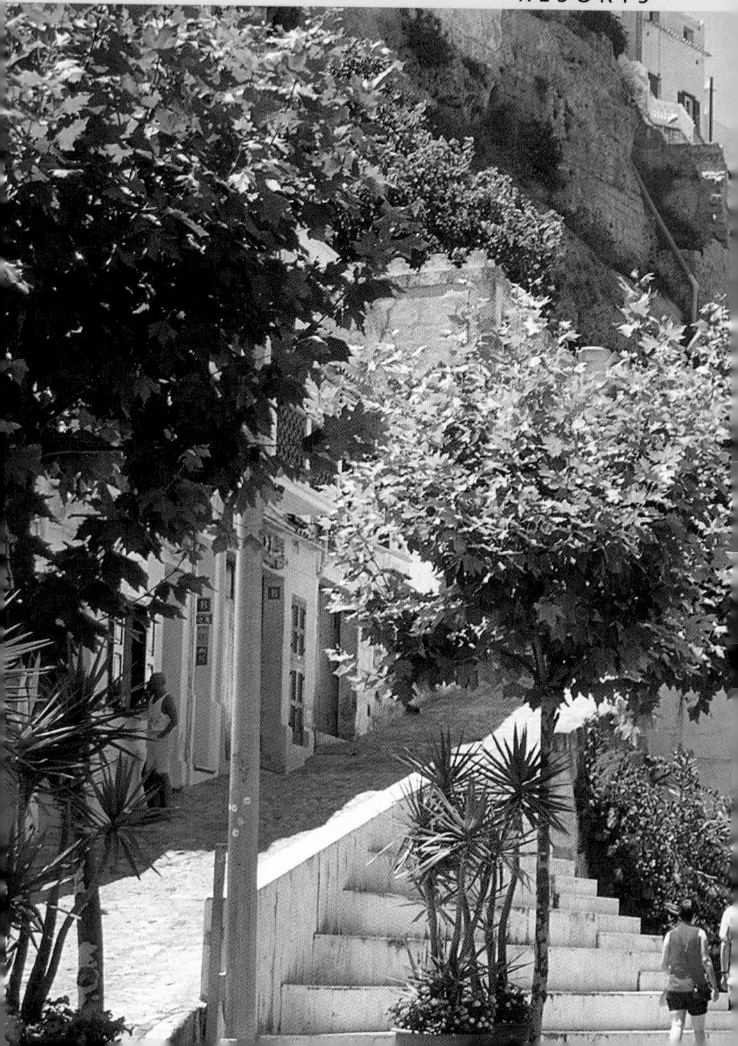

Maó's seafront avenue

Cala Llonga

SHOPPING

There are several shops selling good ceramics and other Menorcan souvenirs along the waterfront at Maó.

Maó harbour and Es Castell

The harbour, which is 5 km long and 1 km at its widest point, is the second largest natural harbour in the world after Pearl Harbor. Due to this fact, and its location in the Mediterranean, it has been a natural strategic stronghold for many nations throughout history. Today, its cruise ships, naval vessels, fishing boats and numerous luxury yachts can be viewed from one of the vantage points, such as Plaça Miranda.

The best way to see the harbour is to join one of the boat tours that leave regularly from both Maó and Es Castell. The guides point out the famous buildings lining the banks, such as Golden Farm, the plum-red Georgian mansion high on the northern shore, where Lord Nelson, the British admiral, is supposed to have stayed with Lady Hamilton, his mistress, and one of Richard Branson's holiday homes. Out in the harbour are three islands: the first, Illa del Rei ('King's Island'), is where Alfonso III landed in 1287 to capture Menorca from the Moors. The British later built a hospital here and renamed it 'Bloody Island'. Further out, watching over the harbour, is La Mola, a Spanish military base at the most easterly point in Spain.

On the other side of the harbour, the old British garrison town of **Es Castell**, also previously known as Villacarlos by the Spanish and Georgetown by the British, contains many Georgian buildings – especially round the main square, Plaça de S'Esplanada. The former barracks contains an interesting **military museum** (*Plaça de S'Esplanada; open 1100–1300 Mon and Thurs and first Sun of each month; admission free*). The harbour at Cales Fonts here is perfectly placed to catch the afternoon sun and many people come here to eat at the numerous harbourside restaurants, both at lunchtime and in the evenings.

 Although lunch in Spain does not usually start much before 1400, arrive early to snap up one of the harbourside tables in Maó or Es Castell.

MÁO HARBOUR

ES CASTELL

Cala Figuera

C de Cala Figuera

Carrer de Corea

Moll de Llevant

Passeig Marítim

Fort de l'Eau

Av Port de Maó

Carrer de Madrid

Fort de l'Eau

C. de Mallorca

Carrer de Bellavista

Carrer del Carme

Carrer Sant Lluís Gonçaga

Carrer de Borja Moll

Carrer de Sant Manuel

Police Station

Camí des Castell

Carrer de la Infanta

Carrer de Gràcia

PORT DE MAÓ

C. General / C. Moret

Police Station

Carrer de S'Arraval

Parc d'es Freginal

Carrer S R I Cajal

Carrer es Còs de Gràcia

C. sa Sínia Costabella

Carrer de Sant Josep

Carrer Rovellada de Dalt

Plaça de s'Esplanada

Carrer Josep Ansel Clavé

Carrer de Pedra Maria Cardona

Avinguda de la

Carrer de Ciutadella

Av José M Quadrado

Carrer de M Lluïsa Serra

LA MOLA
CALA MESQUIDA
CAP ROIG

Xoriguer

C. del Cronista Riudavets

Avinguda de Vives Llull

THINGS TO SEE AND DO

Harbour tours ***
These leave frequently from the waterfront at Maó and from Cales Fonts in Es Castell. Some of the tours use glass-bottomed boats, allowing you to see deep beneath the water.

Fort Marlborough ***
This British-built fortress, near the entrance to Maó harbour at picturesque Cala de Sant Esteve, has recently been restored and opened as a tourist attraction. You can walk along underground tunnels still smelling of gunpowder, enjoying the special effects – including the odd explosion. *Tel: 971 360462. Open Tues–Sat 1000–1300 & 1700–2000, Sun 1000–1330. Closed Mon. Admission free.*

Xoriguer *
Visit this gin distillery on the waterfront at Maó to see the old-fashioned copper stills and taste a wide range of gin-based liqueurs. *Moll de Ponent 93. Tel: 971 362197. Open Mon–Fri 0800–1900, Sat 0900–1300. Closed Sun. Admission free.*

BEACHES
There are no beaches anywhere in Maó harbour. The nearest is at Cala Mesquida, signposted from the road between Maó and La Mola. The beach here, and the Cap Roig fish restaurant on the cliffs, are popular weekend retreats for the people of Maó. There are no facilities on the beach.

RESTAURANTS AND BARS *(see maps on pages 28 and 30)*

All the restaurants along the harbours both in Maó and Es Castell are worth a visit depending on your taste and size of your pocket! There are a variety of gastronomical delights from local Menorcan cuisine to Italian, Indian and Chinese; serving anything from a snack to a 5- or 6-course speciality. The following (see page 31) are worthy of note.

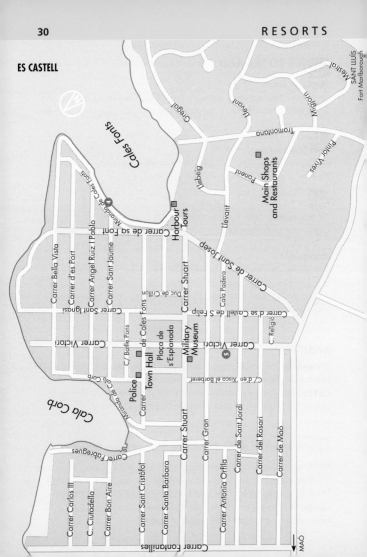

ES CASTELL

Cales Fonts

Cala Corb

SANT LLUIS
Fort Marlborough

Mestral

Migjorn

Tramontana

Pintor Vives

Gregal

Main Shops
and Restaurants

Ponent

Llebeig

Llevant

Pintor Vives

Miranda de Cales Fonts

Harbour
Tours

Carrer de sa Font

Carrer Bella Vista

Carrer d'es Port

Carrer Angel Ruiz I Pablo

Carrer Sant Jaume

Carrer Sant Ignasi

Duc de Crillon

Carrer Stuart

Carrer de Sant Josep

Cala Padera

Carrer d'se Castell de S Felip

C. Religió

Carrer Victori

C/ Balle Pons

Police

Town Hall

Plaça de
s'Esplanada

Military
Museum

Carrer Victori

Carrer de Cales Fons

Miranda de Cala Corb

Carrer Fabregues

Carrer Stuart

Carrer Carlos III

C. Ciutadella

Carrer Bon Aire

Carrer Sant Cristòfol

Carrer Santa Barbara

Carrer Gran

Carrer Antonia Oñfla

Carrer de Sant Jordi

Carrer del Rosari

Carrer de Maó

C/ d'en Xisco el Barberet

Carrer Fontanilles

MAÓ

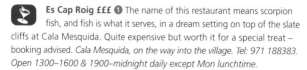

Es Cap Roig £££ ❶ The name of this restaurant means scorpion fish, and fish is what it serves, in a dream setting on top of the slate cliffs at Cala Mesquida. Quite expensive but worth it for a special treat – booking advised. *Cala Mesquida, on the way into the village. Tel: 971 188383. Open 1300–1600 & 1900–midnight daily except Mon lunchtime.*

La Minerva £££ ❷ Part floating restaurant, part converted warehouse with top-notch Spanish dishes, such as steak with *foie gras*, and salmon with pink peppercorns. *Moll de Llevant 87, Maó. Tel: 971 351995. Open 1300–1630 & 2000–2330.*

Roma £ ❸ Popular pizza and pasta restaurant beside the moorings. *Moll de Llevant 295, Cala Figuera, Maó. Tel: 971 353777. Open 1200–0200.*

Ca'n Delio ££ ❹ What could be more romantic than eating fresh grilled sardines and drinking chilled wine beside the sea on a summer evening? *Cales Fones 38, Es Castell. Tel: 971 351711. Open 1230–1530 & 1900–0030.*

Bar España £ ❺ Extremely popular with the locals and visitors alike – try the soufflé sweet! Air-conditioned. *Calle Victori 48–50, Es Castell. Tel: 971 363299. Open daily.*

NIGHTLIFE

Es Castell Local musicians gather at **Es Cau**, a bar set inside a fishermen's cave in the tiny harbour of Cala Corb. For a more refined atmosphere, try the **Piano Bar** at Carrer Sant Ignasi 11 or **Chéspir** cocktail bar on the waterfront at Cales Font 47. The disco pub **Mamas and Papas** always attracts a lively late-night crowd with karaoke from 2300–0400.

Maó harbour The area at the foot of the harbour steps from Maó is a busy late-night meeting place with several fashionable bars. For the latest sounds try **Akelarre**, **Pub Salsa**, **Galileo Galilei**, **Café Baixamar** or **Icaro**, which are all close together on Moll de Ponent. **Nashville** (**££**), at Moll de Llevant 143, has German beer, food and live music some nights until 0400.

Mambo, also at Moll de Llevant, is a highly popular late-night music bar. For those who like a flutter, try the **Casino Maritim**, open until 0400.

S'Algar, Cala Alcaufar and Punta Prima – picturesque and peaceful

The stretch of rocky coastline running along Menorca's south-eastern shore is indented with pretty coves. There are few high-rise buildings and much of the area is still wild. This is where you will find some of Menorca's most peaceful and stylish resorts – including S'Algar, Cala Alcaufar and Punta Prima.

Punta Prima, at the island's south-eastern tip, was appropriately named Sandy Bay by the British during their domination of the island. The resort here has long been a popular holiday spot among Menorcans. Purpose-built S'Algar (pronounced 'Sal-*gar*') possesses some of the best sporting facilities on the island and a mini-train for the kids but, regrettably, no beach. Nearby Cala Alcaufar (pronounced 'Alco-*far*') is a tiny, relaxing resort, ideal for those who wish to enjoy the peace and tranquillity of rural Menorca.

Just inland from the coast is Sant Lluís, a dazzling village of whitewashed houses founded by the French in 1756. In the surrounding countryside, you can still see some of the ancient farmhouses that once surrounded the village.

 TIP! Not only is the S'Algar mini-train fun for children, but it provides a useful means of transport for adults too, with stops at all the key hotels, the S'Algar Sports complex, and the shops, bars and restaurants of the Commercial Centre.

BEACHES

The largest beach in south-eastern Menorca is at Punta Prima, looking across to the tiny island of Isla de l'Aire, uninhabited except for a rare species of black lizard. The lovely sandy beach which gently shelves into the crystal-clear waters of the pretty, cliff-lined bay at Cala Alcaufar makes it a popular choice for families and non-swimmers. Both beaches have sunbeds and parasols for hire, and also pedalos at Punta Prima.

Opposite: Cala Alcaufar

THINGS TO SEE AND DO

Hippódrome de Maó **
Maó's racetrack is situated just outside Sant Lluís, and popular trotting races (*see page 118*) are held on Saturday evenings at around 1800. *Carretera Maó–Sant Lluís.*

Horse riding *
Fun for all the family! Take ponies for a trot along the leafy paths or ride them in the pony school. *Club Hipic Es Boeret, S'Algar. Tel: 971 151049.*

Molí de Dalt **
This blue and white windmill, at the entrance to Sant Lluís from Maó, is now a museum with a collection of old farming tools. It is also an information centre. *Tel: 971 151084. Open Mon–Fri mornings and evenings, Sat mornings only.*

S'Algar Sports **
An extensive complex offering a wide range of sports from mountain biking, sailing and kayaking to tennis, mini-golf, archery and bowls. There's a daily Kid's Club 1000–1300 and 1500–1730. *Club Hotel Sant Lluis. Tel: 971 359454. You need to reserve the activities 24 hours beforehand at the Info-desk opposite La Raqueta café.*

Watersports **
Try your hand at diving, water-skiing or sailing. *Passeig Marítim, S'Algar. Tel: 971 150610.*

RESTAURANTS AND BARS

Las Palmeras ££ This popular pizzeria-grill restaurant is part of the Las Palmeras apartment complex. Children can swim in the pool, while adults eat. *S'Algar. Tel: 971 150603. Open 1100–1530 & 1900–2300.*

Pan y Vino £££ Stylish British-run restaurant in a 200-year-old farmhouse in the charming hamlet of Torret, between Punta Prima and Sant Lluís. Booking is essential. *Camí de la Coixa 3, Torret. Tel: 971 150322. Open 2000–2300.*

La Rueda £ Busy village restaurant and *tapas* bar on the main street of Sant Lluís. The locals come here to eat fried squid rings, Galician octopus and meatballs in tomato sauce. Portions are small and reasonably priced, so order several. *Carrer Sant Lluís 30, Sant Lluís. Tel: 971 150349. Open 1300–1530 & 1930–2330.*

 La Venta £££ Excellent restaurant opposite the roundabout, ample parking across road. *Avinguda Sa Pau, 158, Sant Lluís. Tel: 971 150995. Open 1300–1530 & 1930–2330. Closed Mon lunchtime.*

Xuroy £ Enjoy freshly grilled fish or a snack salad in this idyllic setting beside the beach at Cala Alcaufar. *Tel: 971 151820. Open 1300–1500 & 1930–2200.*

NIGHTLIFE

Why not? Popular karaoke bar on the fringes of the resort in an attractive garden setting. *S'Algar. Open 2200–0300.*

Binibeca Vell and Es Canutells –
award-winning architecture

The rocky coast from Binibeca to Es Canutells boasts some of Menorca's finest seascapes with its numerous small, sandy beaches lined with attractive holiday developments. The star attraction is undoubtedly Binibeca Vell, with an award-winning, Moorish-style complex designed as a modern fishing village.

The 'fishing village' of Binibeca Vell attracted international attention when it was designed by Antonio Sintes, the Spanish architect, in 1972. Until then, Menorca's tourist resorts had consisted mostly of high-rise hotels – but Binibeca was consciously different, a dazzling village of whitewashed cottages (even the roofs are painted white!) with wooden balconies lining a veritable maze of narrow alleyways around a small fishing harbour. It has often been imitated, but never bettered, and Menorca's coastline is starting to look very different as a result of Sintes' inspiration.

Just a short walk along the coast to the east are the neighbouring resorts of Binibeca Nou and Cala Torret.

 Get up early (or stay up late) to watch the sun rise over Binibeca beach – then pop into Sant Lluís on a Sunday, when the bars fill with locals tucking into platefuls of *tapas* after church.

BEACHES
Binibeca beach, between Binibeca Vell and Cala Torret, has shallow water, clean sand, and a beach bar renting out sunshades, loungers and pedalos, making it very popular for families. From the car park, a path leads through the pine trees to a shaded picnic area in the cove. There is also excellent wheelchair access to the beach.

SHOPPING

The *complejo turístico* (tourist complex) of Binibeca Vell contains several small, quality shops.

THINGS TO DO

Watersports **

The Centro de Buceo (diving centre) at Cala Torret runs courses in scuba diving as well as snorkelling tours by boat. *Cala Torret. Tel: 971 188528.*

RESTAURANTS & BARS

 Binigrill ££ Family restaurant on the main square of the 'fishing village', serving grills, steaks and fresh fish. *Binibeca Vell. Tel: 971 150594. Open 1000–1600 & 1900–2330.*

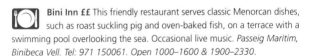 **Bini Inn ££** This friendly restaurant serves classic Menorcan dishes, such as roast suckling pig and oven-baked fish, on a terrace with a swimming pool overlooking the sea. Occasional live music. *Passeig Maritim, Binibeca Vell. Tel: 971 150061. Open 1000–1600 & 1900–2330.*

 Los Bucaneros £ This shack on Binibeca beach has probably the best setting of any restaurant in Menorca – the perfect place to eat fresh grilled fish just yards from the sea. *Open 1030–2000.*

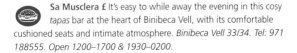 **DP £** Busy, family restaurant with hearty portions of Spanish and English cooking on a covered terrace overlooking a pretty cove. *Cala Torret. Tel: 971 651037. Open 1030–2230. Closed Wed.*

Sa Musclera £ It's easy to while away the evening in this cosy *tapas* bar at the heart of Binibeca Vell, with its comfortable cushioned seats and intimate atmosphere. *Binibeca Vell 33/34. Tel: 971 188555. Open 1200–1700 & 1930–0200.*

Es Canutells

Following the coast road west from Binibeca you pass many rocky coves and small beaches like Binisafuller, Biniparratx and Binidali, all worth a visit. Es Canutells is now a mixture of private villas and a holiday complex. There is a good sandy beach situated at the mouth of a gorge, protected from the sea by high cliffs.

San Clemente ***

Just inland from Binibeca and Es Canutells is the charming market village of San Clemente with its unexpected English inns and an excellent music bar, famed throughout the island for its live jazz.

RESTAURANTS AND BARS

 Canutells-Playa £ Feast on the freshest of fish, a salad, *crêpe* or omelette on the shaded terrace of this snack bar overlooking the beach. There's also a children's menu and a take-away service. *Cala Canutells. Tel: 971 188934. Open 0900–0030.*

Casino de San Clemente £ Popular village restaurant and *tapas* bar which doubles up as a music pub, with live jazz on Tuesdays (from 2130) and ballroom dancing on Saturday nights. Visitors are welcome to bring their own instruments to the jazz sessions. *Carrer Sant Jaume 4, San Clemente. Tel: 971 153418. Open Thurs–Tues 1230–1600 & 1930–2330. Closed Wed.*

Coach and Horses ££ Once inside this pub you could be in an English village. Sandwiches, snacks, hot meals and English beers. *Carrer Sant Jaume 38, San Clemente. Tel: 971 153334. Open 1100–1600 & 1900–midnight.*

Es Molí de Foc £££ This up-market Spanish and French restaurant has a garden which is just right for a romantic candlelit dinner. The specialities include duck breast with strawberry sauce and three different kinds of *paella. Booking advised. Carrer de Sant Llorenç 65, San Clemente. Tel: 971 153222. Open 1200–2300. Closed Mon lunchtime and all day Sun.*

The Three Horseshoes £ English pub in a back street of San Clemente serving typical English food and a wide range of imported beers. The theme nights here include quizzes on Mondays. *Carrer de Sant Llorenç 36, San Clemente. Tel: 971 153024. Open 1100–1600 & 1900–late. Closed Mon and Tues lunchtimes.*

Es Canutells

El Pueblo de Pescadores, the fishing village, Binibeca Vell

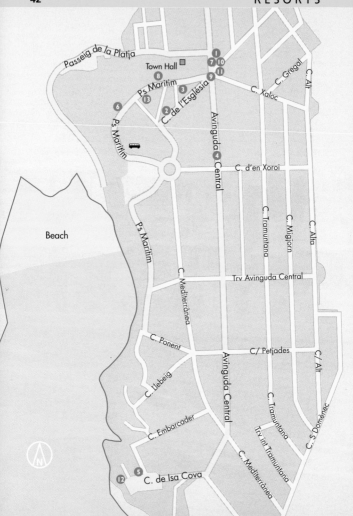

Cala'n Porter –
Menorca's first beach resort

The setting of Cala'n Porter is magnificent – tall, pine-studded cliffs to either side of a wide sandy beach, with a stream tumbling out of a limestone gorge to run across the beach into a crystal-clear sea. The cliffs on the east side are home to restaurants, shops and bars, while those on the west are still totally undeveloped.

The best views in Cala'n Porter are from the Cova d'en Xoroi, a natural cave in the cliff face which acts as a bar by day and a disco by night (*see page 47*). The cave is the setting for one of Menorca's most enduring folk legends. The story goes that Xoroi, a one-eared Moorish pirate, was shipwrecked at Cala'n Porter and hid inside this cave. One night, while searching for food at a nearby farm, he kidnapped a beautiful maiden. They lived together inside the cave for many years and she bore him three children, but one day Xoroi's footprints in the winter snow gave away his hiding place. To avoid capture, Xoroi and his son leapt into the sea, never to be seen again.

A steep flight of steps connects the main street to the beach – but once you have gone down, you do not have to climb back up – you could always come up in the mini-train instead.

THINGS TO SEE AND DO

Cales Coves **
This pair of rocky coves just east of Cala'n Porter is best known for its many burial caves which were carved out of the rock in ancient times. More than 2,000 years ago the dead and the living would be found here side by side.

SHOPPING

Ca N'Andreu This shop has a good selection of souvenirs, including pottery, jewellery, carved olive wood and Menorca T-shirts. *Carrer Xaloc 3. Open 1000–1330 & 1700–2200.*

Spar This centrally located supermarket stocks everything from Heinz baked beans and English newspapers to blow-up whales. *Avinguda Central. Open Mon–Sat 0800–2100, Sun 0800–1400 & 1600–1800.*

BEACHES

On the beach at Cala'n Porter you can hire sunbeds, beach umbrellas and pedalos here and there is a handful of beachside restaurants and bars. From the eastern cliffs, near the Cova d'en Xoroi, a path leads to two small shingle beaches at Cales Coves (*see page 43*), where there is good snorkelling and swimming from the rocks.

RESTAURANTS AND BARS (see map on page 42)

Aloha £ ❶ Every customer receives a garland in this Hawaiian-style cocktail bar in a bamboo hut on the edge of town. The music includes karaoke parties once a week and cabarets on Sundays at 2100. *Carrer Xaloc. Tel: 971 377028. Open 2030 till late.*

Seagram's ££ ❷ Tired of *paella* and grilled sardines? Ring the changes with BBQ ribs, *fajitas* and deep-pan pizzas at this American-style 'eating and watering hole'. *Carrer Mediterraneo 13. Tel: 971 377359. Open 1200–midnight.*

Lorengo £ ❸ Friendly family restaurant serving international cuisine with a Spanish twist. *Passeig Marítim 5. Tel: 971 377196. Open 1000–1600 & 1800–midnight.*

Napoli £ ❹ The pizzeria in the Siesta Mar apartment complex has live music (flamenco and Brazilian dancing) most evenings. *Avinguda Central. Tel: 971 317411. Open 0900–midnight.*

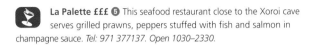

La Palette £££ ❺ This seafood restaurant close to the Xoroi cave serves grilled prawns, peppers stuffed with fish and salmon in champagne sauce. *Tel: 971 377137. Open 1030–2330.*

El Patio £ ❻ Friendly, Scottish-run restaurant serving good-value British food. The bar has satellite TV and a wide range of imported beers. *Passeig Marítim 4. Tel: 971 377206. Open 1100–1500 & 1900–0300.*

El Pulpo ££ ❼ The name of this restaurant means 'the octopus' and the speciality is seafood, served on a shady terrace beneath the palm trees. There is occasional live music. *Avinguda Central 347. Tel: 971 377110. Open 1200–1600 & 1900–midnight.*

La Salamandra ££ ❽ Family orientated restaurant, with swings for the children, on a large terrace just off the main street. The bar attached to the restaurant has a loud late-night disco. *Passeig Marítim. Tel: 971 377453. Open 1200–midnight.*

Sa Paissa ££ ❾ Popular family restaurant in the centre of the resort with an extensive menu of home-cooked food including a good choice of vegetarian dishes and a children's menu. It also has a swimming pool with sunbeds. *Avinguda Central. Tel: 971 377389. Open 0900–2330. Web: www.sapaissa.com, e-mail: sapaissa@sapaissa.com.*

Southern Fried Chicken £ ❿ Chicken, hamburgers, BBQ ribs, hot dogs and pizzas. Eat in or take-away. *Avinguda Central, Cala'n Porter – opposite Sa Paissa. Open 1200–0030.*

Village Pub £ ⓫ A typical British pub, decorated with fishing nets, and open all day serving everything from full English breakfasts to good-value main meals, such as shepherd's pie and toad-in-the-hole. *Carrer Xaloc 24. At the top of Passeig Marítim. Tel: 971 377129. Open 0900–2300.*

NIGHTLIFE

Cova d'en Xoroi ⑫
After nightfall this popular lookout spot (*open 1100–2100; admission charge*) turns into a disco, with everything from soul to rave music on a dance floor perched above the sea. A good place to watch the moon come up – and maybe the sun too. *Open 2300 to dawn. Admission charge.*

Stop ⑬ Cocktail bar where the young and trendy hang out late at night – loud music and a great *sangria*. *Passeig Marítim. Open 2100–0500.*

Pick of the beaches – Cala'n Porter

Son Bou – Menorca's longest beach

About 2 miles (3km) of pale golden sand, between a pair of rocky headlands, make Son Bou the longest beach on Menorca. The eastern end of the beach, where the hotels and shops are found, is always busy – but, as you go west, the beach becomes wilder, backed by sand dunes and freshwater marshes, which support a large population of migrant birds.

The resort has all the facilities you need for a seaside holiday – beach bars hiring out sunbeds, shops selling buckets and spades, safe swimming, and opportunities for windsurfing and water-skiing. Behind the marshes is the Club San Jaime, an entertainment centre at the heart of a tourist village, with restaurants and bars, a water-slide for children and a disco at night (*see below*).

Visitors have been drawn to Son Bou for literally thousands of years, and the prehistoric remains on the beach and in the nearby countryside are fascinating reminders of Menorca's history. As you stumble across the ruins of ancient churches and watch-towers, it is interesting to wonder what the visitors of 2,000 years' time will make of today's apartments and beach bars.

 Climb up to the cave houses in the cliffs above the prehistoric basilica for the best views along Son Bou beach. And don't forget to take your camera!

THINGS TO SEE AND DO

Club San Jaime *
The winding water-chute here is the most thrilling on Menorca and children are guaranteed to want to go on it again and again. There is also an unusual wooden labyrinth, Amaze'n'Maze, whose interlocking patterns change every week. Adults can eat, swim or relax in the beautifully landscaped gardens

whose views stretch over the marshes and down to the sea. *In the Club San Jaime apartment complex. Open 1000–2200. Water-slides open from 1000–1700, maze from 1130–2200.*

Paleo-Christian basilica **

The remains of this 5th-century church were discovered hidden in the sand in 1951 and are now enclosed by a low stone wall. You can walk right around the outside, peering in at the ancient stone pillars and the enormous baptismal font, carved from a single block of stone. The basilica is found at the east end of the beach beneath the two large hotels.

Torre d'en Gaumes **

This prehistoric settlement, dating from 1500BC, is about 3 miles (5km) outside Son Bou and reached from the main road to Alaior. A footpath leads right around the site, which includes three well-preserved *talaiots* (circular watch-towers), a broken *taula*, or altar, and an ingenious water collection system. The views back down to the sea are spectacular. At one time this 'village' was home to 1,000 people and it may once have been the capital of Menorca.

BEACHES

Only one – but what a beach! As you head west from the two big hotels, the beach becomes quieter and there are far fewer people wearing far fewer clothes. The western half of the beach is unofficially nudist. If you tire of Son Bou, a half-hour walk from the western end leads around the headland to another fine beach at Sant Tomàs (*see page 54*).

RESTAURANTS AND BARS

Boni ££ The speciality is seafood at this old-world restaurant and pizzeria with wooden seats and a great view of the sea. Order the mixed seafood grill and you will have enough for two. *Centro Comercial. Tel: 971 372277. Open 1100–midnight.*

Bou Hai £ Hawaiian-style cocktail bar where some of the waiters wear roller-skates. The menu includes fresh watermelon, pear and carrot juices as well as alcoholic drinks. *Centro Comercial. Tel: 971 371572. Open 1200–0300.*

Casa Andres ££ Friendly local restaurant featuring omelettes, pasta, steaks and salads. *Centro Comercial. Tel: 971 371918. Open 1200–midnight.*

 Copacabana ££ Disco and Cocktail Bar, Son Bou. Wonderful views over the coast. *Open 1630–0330.*

 El Jardin ££ This restaurant beside the swimming pool in the Club San Jaime complex specialises in grilled meats and pasta dishes. Eat here when your children have finished playing on the water-slides next door. *Club San Jaime. Tel: 971 372000. Open 0900–midnight.*

 Il Gondoliere £££ Smart, popular pizzeria and Italian restaurant. *Urbanizacion San Jaime. Tel: 971 372000. Open 1830–2300.*

 Las Dunas £ A good selection of international cuisine, such as prawn cocktail, spaghetti and roast lamb, at this friendly terrace restaurant close to the beach. *Centro Comercial. Tel: 971 371665. Open 0900–midnight.*

 Sa Fruita £ This comfortable, modern bar serves *paella*, pizzas, ice-creams and snacks throughout the day. *Centro Comercial. Tel: 971 371375. Open 1000–midnight.*

 Son Bou ££ Salmon, steaks, sandwiches and a good children's menu are served on a shady terrace in the resort's main shopping centre. *Centro Comercial. Tel: 971 372503. Open 1000–midnight.*

NIGHTLIFE

Club San Jaime The disco inside the San Jaime apartment complex plays a wide range of music to appeal to all ages and tastes. *Open midnight–0600. Admission free.*

Son Bou This disco is the place to be on Thursday nights, for its strawberry aphrodisiac foam parties, or for techno fans on Fridays and Saturdays. *Centro Comercial. Open 2300–0400. Admission charge.*

Sant Tomàs –
dunes and pine woods

Sant Tomàs (Santo Tomas in Spanish) is the smallest and quietest of the main south coast resorts, reached by a beautiful drive through pine woods from the village of Es Migjorn Gran. Everything at Sant Tomàs is centred on a single main street, with apartments, shops and restaurants to either side and the beach just a short walk away between the sand dunes.

The attraction here is the superb beach, covered in soft white sand and perfect for swimming or sunbathing. But if it looks too good to be true, it is – a freak storm in 1989 removed all of the sand and what you lie on today has had to be imported.

Es Migjorn Gran, with its pastel-coloured cottages in a maze of narrow streets, is a good place to soak up the atmosphere of a rural Menorcan town. The main square, Sa Plaça, is lined with bars and cafés as well as the parish church of St Christopher. This simple cream and white church, with its bell tower topped by a cockerel, looks much more Greek than Spanish and the whole town has a classic Mediterranean feel.

The unspoiled beaches beyond the Bar Es Bruc reach right up to the fields and a walk here can make a pleasant change – but be warned: the second beach, Binigaus, is very popular with nudists.

THINGS TO SEE AND DO

Pony Club *
This pony farm, hidden in the pinewoods behind Sant Tomàs, offers riding lessons and can hire out ponies for rides. *Tel: 971 370370.*

SHOPPING

Galeria Migjorn is owned by the British watercolour artist Graham Byfield and has exhibitions of his work and that of other local artists. *Carrer Sant Llorenç 12, Es Migjorn Gran. Tel: 971 370364. Open Mon–Sat 1000–1300 & 1900–2100.*

BEACHES

The main beach at Sant Tomàs is one of the best on the island – you can hire sunbeds, umbrellas and pedalos here, and there are also a couple of good bars. At the west end, beyond Bar Es Bruc, the beach becomes known as Sant Adeodato; beyond this, past the rocky island offshore, is Binigaus beach, where swimming is not recommended because of the currents. From the other end of Sant Tomàs's beach you can walk to the beach at Son Bou (*see page 50*).

RESTAURANTS AND BARS

Es Bruc £ Beach bar with simple food, such as sausages and burgers, and wonderful views out to sea. *San Adeodato. Tel: 971 370488. Open 1000–midnight.*

Ca Na Pilar ££ The locals frequent this restaurant for its imaginative Menorcan home cooking. *Booking advised. Carretera Es Mercadal, Es Migjorn Gran. Tel: 971 370212. Open 1300–1500 & 2000–2300.*

Chic ££ This *tapas* bar with a pretty garden terrace, in the heart of Es Migjorn Gran, is popular with locals and visitors alike. Choose from a wide range of traditional appetisers. *Carrer Major 71, Es Migjorn Gran. Tel: 971 370129. Open Tues–Sat 1200–1500 (except Aug), Tues–Sun 1800–midnight. Closed Mon.*

Costa Sur ££ This restaurant on the roof of Sant Tomàs's shopping centre is the place to come for that special night out. More formal than most resort restaurants, it serves classic Spanish dishes, such as salmon and roast lamb, in an elegant dining room or on the shady terrace outside. *Platja Sant Tomàs. Tel: 971 370326. Open 1900–midnight.*

Las Dunas £ Popular family restaurant, with pool tables, crazy golf, evening entertainment and a mini-disco for kids. The food is mostly pizzas and pasta dishes. *Platja Sant Tomàs. Tel: 971 370370. Open 1230–1530 & 1830–2300.*

58 S'Engolidor ££ This family-run restaurant on a garden terrace behind a small Menorcan townhouse only has a few tables, so booking is essential. The food is traditional Menorcan, and the views are superb. *Carrer Major 3, Es Migjorn Gran. Tel: 971 370193. Open Tues–Sun 2000–2300. Closed Mon.*

Nikos Bar £ This open-air bar is Sant Tomàs's meeting place, where everyone gathers around the pool at night to hear Nikos play the blues. Snacks, such as chicken and chips, at lunchtime, but drinks only in the evening. *Mestral Apartments. Tel: 971 370370. Open 1100–midnight.*

Es Pins ££ A romantic and special place – a fish restaurant overlooking the beach, with friendly service and fantastic views. Try the seafood *paella. Tel: 971 370541. Platja Sant Tomàs. Open 1030–2330.*

La Ribera ££ This friendly café near the Riu Nelson hotel serves a breakfast buffet from 0830 to 1030 and generous portions of hearty Spanish dishes, such as rabbit with snails, for lunch. *Platja Sant Tomàs. Open 0830–1030, 1230–1530 & 1830–2300.*

NIGHTLIFE

Admirals Pub This busy nightclub on the first floor of the Hotel Victoria Playa plays a mixture of gentle pop and rave music. In July and August it is packed out with teenagers but at other times it is popular with people of all ages. *Platja Sant Tomàs. Tel: 971 370200. Open 2300–0300.*

Malibu Hawaiian-style beach bar with straw roof and parasols, a popular late-night spot which stays open until around 0500. *Platja Sant Tomàs. Open 1000–0500.*

Victory Club This smart disco, decked out with tartan, portholes and prints of Nelson, attracts all ages and plays all the latest sounds. *Platja Sant Tomàs. Tel: 971 370125. Open 2215–0300.*

← ALGENDAR GORGE

Centre Commercial

Avinguda de Sa Punta

MIRADOR DE SA PUNTA

Carretera de Sta Galdana a Ferreries

Passeig del Riu

Carrer del Riu

Riu de Santa Galdana

Mirador des Riu

①

⑦

②

Carrer de Llevent

Carrer de la Serpentona

Carrer de l'Ermita

Carrer de la Ladera

MEDITERRANEAN SEA

Playa de Sta Galdana

④

⑥

Passeig del Riu

Centre Commercial

③

⑤

Costa des Mirador

Passaie Inferior

Carrer de la Serpentona

Carrer de la Pina

Ⓜ

Cala Galdana – queen of the coves

Cala Galdana – also known as Santa Galdana – has been called the 'queen of Menorca's coves' and its setting is quite spectacular. A river runs across the beach beside a horseshoe of golden sand, nestling between tall limestone cliffs and pine trees reflected in the sea. Many people think this is the most beautiful spot on Menorca's entire coast.

Until recently there was not even a road here – but now Cala Galdana has grown into a busy resort, with villas and apartments climbing up the hillsides and enough facilities to keep everyone happy. The dramatic scenery of the bay and the south coast can be viewed from vantage points on the clifftops, while the wide beach, with its calm water and gently shelving sand, is ideal for swimming. There are several beach bars, a wide range of watersports, plus mini-golf and a water-slide for the children. Cala Galdana is also a good base for gentle walks, to some of the quieter coves along this stretch of coastline, or inland between the walls of the Algendar Gorge (*see below*).

 An hour-long walk through pine-scented woods leads to the delightful cove of Cala Macarella. There's no need to take a picnic – the Café Susy is right on the beach and will even rent out parasols and sunbeds.

THINGS TO SEE AND DO

Algendar Gorge **

This deep limestone gorge, with a marshy river running along its valley, begins where the road runs out behind the Hotel Cala Galdana. Walk along the banks of the gorge for wonderful views, especially at sunset. In spring and early summer the gorge buzzes with butterflies, birds and wild flowers.

Viewpoints **

Two lookout points above Cala Galdana both offer spectacular views. The **Mirador des Riu** looks down over the Algendar river and gorge, while the **Mirador de Sa Punta** gives sweeping views of the entire bay and right across the sea to Mallorca. Both *miradors* can be reached by car or by climbing the steep steps from the beach.

Watersports **

Motorboats, dinghies, windsurfing boards and snorkelling equipment can all be hired on the beach, along with canoes and pedalos. Diving lessons are available from the Submorena diving school, near the Hotel Cala Galdana.

 The Cala Gandana Express mini-train is a fun and relaxing way to explore the resort – and it takes you to some spectacular viewpoints. *Departures every 45 minutes, 1000–1300 & 1700–2330.*

EXCURSIONS

Boat trips

Glass-bottomed boats make regular trips along the south coast, stopping at the beautiful Cala Trebalúger cove for swimming and a picnic on the beach.

BEACHES

The beach at Cala Galdana has all that you could wish for, but if you want a little more solitude there are several quieter beaches that can be reached on foot.

West of Cala Galdana

The footpath from the Hotel Audax leads to Cala Macarella, where there is a beach bar and several caves cut into the cliffs. Just over the headland is the unspoiled cove of Cala Macarelleta, a lovely hide-away spot and just 40 minutes' walk from Cala Galdana.

East of Cala Galdana

A 20-minute walk from the eastern cliffs takes you to Cala Mitjana, where adventurous swimmers can go right inside the limestone caves. There are no beach facilities here. Cala Mitjana can also be reached by car but you have to pay a toll for crossing private land.

RESTAURANTS AND BARS *(see map on page 56)*

Cala Galdana Playa £ ❶ Friendly poolside bar inside an apartment complex, serving generous portions of Spanish food at very reasonable prices – and with great views of the Algendar Gorge. *Passeig del Riu. Tel: 971 154676. Open 1000–midnight.*

Chiringuito Toni £ ❷ The best of the beach bars, in a quiet setting beneath the cliffs. A very romantic place to eat *paella* as you watch the sun set over the sea. *On the beach. Tel: 971 154632. Open 0900–midnight.*

Don Pepé ££ ❸ This restaurant inside the Hotel Audax serves top-quality Spanish cuisine, specialising in charcoal-grilled meat. There is usually some entertainment laid on during the evening. *Hotel Audax. Tel: 971 154646. Open 1230–1530 &1900–2200.*

El Mirador ££ ❹ Seafood restaurant perched on a rocky outcrop overlooking the beach – from the *miradors* on the hillside you would think this was an island. *Over the footbridge from the Hotel Audax. Tel: 971 154503. Open 1000–late.*

El Rey del Jamón ££ ❺ Typical Spanish bar-restaurant (the name means 'the King of Ham'), half-way up the hill behind the Hotel Audax. The *paella* is good here and the children's menu is excellent value. *Carrer Costa d'es Mirador. Open 1130–0100.*

Tobogán £ ❻ This pizzeria beside the marina is a great place to take kids as it has a water-slide, a playground and a mini-golf course where the children can have fun while you eat. *Platja Cala Galdana. Tel: 971 154616. Open 0830–midnight.*

NIGHTLIFE

Mississippi ❼ Popular late-night venue with pool tables, Sky Sports TV, cocktails and over 20 different types of beer. *Passeig del Riu. Open 1800–0400.*

Cala Galdana

The Marina – focal point of Cala'n Bosch

Cala'n Bosch, Cala Blanca and Cala Santandría –
excellent base for watersports

These three resorts on Menorca's south-west coastline are very different in character. Cala Santandría is little more than a rocky cove, with a handful of restaurants and bars where the people of Ciutadella come at weekends. Cala'n Bosch – also known as Cala En Bosc – is western Menorca's watersports centre and a lively resort with two beaches and a wide choice of entertainment.

Life at Cala'n Bosch revolves around the marina, the starting point for a series of excursions along the unspoiled south coast (*see below*). The smart marina is lined with restaurants and bars where you can sit out of doors soaking up the sun and watching the yachts bob up and down in the water. Nearby Cala Blanca has suffered from excessive development but still has a charming pine-fringed cove lined with popular restaurants and bars. The main beach is just a short walk away.

Cala Santandría is linked to the smaller cove of Sa Caleta, whose beach is overlooked by an old watch-tower. This was the site of a French invasion of Menorca in 1756. Nowadays it is a peaceful spot with a sandy beach at the end of a long inlet and the only invaders are people looking for a place in the sun.

 The cliffs beside the lighthouse at Cap d'Artrutx, close to Cala'n Bosch, are a great place to watch the sun set into the sea with the mountains of Mallorca silhouetted against the sky.

THINGS TO SEE AND DO

Crystal Seas Scuba *

Diving school based at Cala'n Bosch marina and a sailing school on the beach at Son Xoriguer offering tuition in windsurfing and dinghy and catamaran sailing. *Cala'n Bosch Marina 11/12. Tel: 971 387038.*

Surf'n'Sail Menorca *

Sailing, windsurfing, canoeing and water-skiing from Son Xoriguer beach, including special lessons for children aged between 8 and 14. *Watersportcentre Platja Son Xoriguer, Tel: 971 387090.*

Hotel Poseidon *

This hotel beside the beach at Cala Santandría has a scuba-diving school. *Tel: 971 382644.*

EXCURSIONS

Boat trips **

Various excursions are available from the marina taking you along the south coast to swim at unspoiled beaches.

SHOPPING

Centro Comercial, Cala'n Bosch The shopping centre at the north end of the marina has a supermarket, gift shops, a chemist and the Torres shop, selling handmade Menorcan leather shoes.

Hiper Cuitadella Out-of-town hypermarket on the road to Cala'n Bosch and Sa Caleta, just outside Ciutadella. *Open Mon–Sat 0900–2100, Sun 0900–1400.*

BEACHES

The beach at Cala'n Bosch is wide and sandy and deepens only gradually, making it safe for swimming. A ten-minute walk, or a ride on the mini-train, leads you to another beach at Son Xoriguer, where there are bars, shops and showers, as well as watersports centres. The white sand and safe, shallow water at Cala Blanca makes this beach a popular choice for families. Strong swimmers can explore the sea-caves in the surrounding limestone cliffs. Sa Caleta has a sandy, small beach or you can walk around the cliffs to the slightly larger beach at Cala Santandría.

RESTAURANTS AND BARS

Café Balear ££ Seafood restaurant beside the marina, serving everything from grilled lobster to squid in monkfish sauce. *Cala'n Bosch. Tel: 608 744816. Open 1000–midnight. Closed Mon.*

Es Caliu ££ Large, rustic restaurant, hung with hams, on the main road between Cala'n Bosch and Santandría – the speciality here is charcoal grills. *Carretera Cala Blanca (near the turn-off for Cala Blanca). Tel: 971 380165. Open 1200–1600 & 1900–midnight.*

Ca'n Anglada ££ Friendly restaurant with a wide range of Menorcan specialities – try the special *paella*. *Cala'n Bosch. By the marina. Tel: 971 381402. Open 1200–1330 & 1800–midnight.*

Ca'n Carrio £ Pizzeria on the beach at Cala Santandría – the kids can play in the sand while you eat. *Cala Santandría. Tel: 971 482467. Open 1130–1530 & 1900–midnight.*

China Town £ Menorca's original Cantonese restaurant. *Cala'n Bosch. By the marina. Tel: 971 385706. Open 1730–midnight.*

 Cova Sa Nacra ££ This cool, shady cliffside bar overlooks Cala Santandría. The restaurant serves tasty fish and meat dishes. *Cala Santandría. Tel: 971 386206. Open 1030–0100.*

 Lord Nelson £ Good food and a children's menu in the Sa Caleta Playa apartments. *Tel: 971 481606. Open 0800–midnight.*

 Mirador Beach Club ££ Local cuisine overlooking the beach at Cala Blanca, with barbecues every evening and a swimming pool for the kids. *Cala Blanca. Tel: 971 480478. Open 0900–0300.*

 El Pescador ££ Fresh fish, pizzas, and rides for children – beside the marina at the water's edge. *Cala'n Bosch. Tel: 971 359539. Open 1130–midnight.*

 Pub Britannia £ Very popular British pub, offering live music every evening. Next to El Pescador. *Open 1030–0400.*

 Sa Quadra ££ Top-quality Menorcan cuisine at reasonable prices, with vegetarian and children's menus, and a shady bamboo terrace. *Behind Cala Santandría beach. Tel: 971 480959. Open 1100–midnight.*

NIGHTLIFE

Big Apple Karaoke bar on the edge of Cala'n Bosch. *Carrer de Tramuntana, Cala'n Bosch. Open 1700–0400. Disco from midnight.*

Dreams Anything goes at this nightclub, which is popular with both locals and visitors. The theme nights include a weekly foam party on Fridays. Over-18s only. *Carrer de S'Abellarol 17. Cala Santandría. Open 2000–0500. Admission charge.*

Moonlight It would be hard to find a more romantic venue for a cocktail bar, overlooking a tiny cove. *Avinguda Cala Blanca. Open 1000–0300.*

Cala'n Bruch and Cala'n Forcat –
fun for all the family

The rugged coastline to the west of Ciutadella is studded with rocky coves and fjord-like inlets of crystal-clear water. This area has grown rapidly in recent years to become one of Menorca's liveliest holiday centres, with a wide choice of restaurants, bars and nightlife. At the same time, just inland, you can still see the fields dotted with dry-stone sheep-shelters like pyramids.

There are four separate coves here – Cala'n Blanes, Cala'n Bruch (also known as Cala En Brut), Cala'n Forcat and Cales Piques (or Calas Picas) – but over the years they have merged into one mega-resort, centred on the Los Delfines complex. Plaça d'Espanya, the square at the heart of Los Delfines, has shops, restaurants and even an open-air chapel. From here it is a short walk to any of the four beaches – and if you don't fancy the walk, you can always hop on to the mini-train which tours the streets at regular intervals. These resorts make a great base for a fun-filled family holiday, with everything you need to keep people of all ages amused – and the city of Ciutadella just a few miles away.

 There are good sunset views from El Patio restaurant, and its neighbour Es Bufador, on the seafront promenade between Cala'n Forcat and Calas Picas.

THINGS TO SEE AND DO

Aquapark **
Swimming pools with slides, crazy golf, open-air jacuzzis, playgrounds, mini-karting, bars and endless other attractions for all the family. *Avinguda de los Delfines. Tel: 971 388251. Open 1000–2200.*

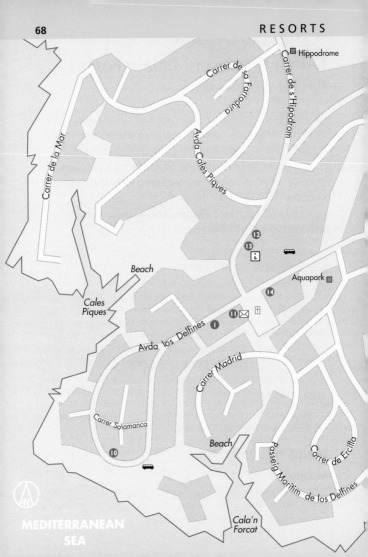

Hippodrome

Carrer de s'Hipodrom

Carrer de sa Farragut

Carrer de la Mar

Avda Cales Piques

12

13

Aquapark

14

Beach

Cales Piques

11 ✉

Avda los Delfines

Carrer Madrid

Carrer Solamanca

Beach

Passeig Marítim de los Delfines

Carrer de Ercilla

10

Cala'n Forcat

MEDITERRANEAN SEA

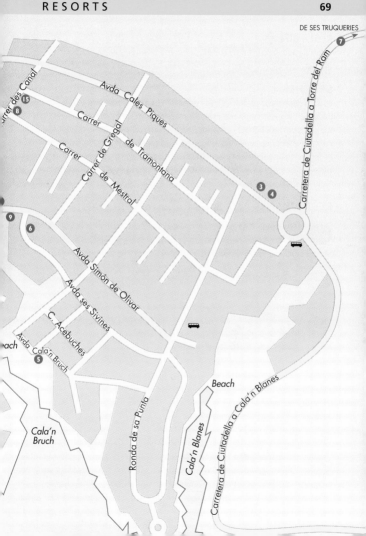

DE SES TRUQUERIES

Carretera de Ciutadella a Torre del Ram

Avda Cales Piques

Carrer des Canal

Carrer

Carrer de Gregal de Tramontana

Carrer de Mestral

Avda Simón de Olivar

Avda ses Sivines

C. Acebuches

Avda Cala'n Bruch

Beach

Cala'n Blanes

Carretera de Ciutadella a Cala'n Blanes

Ronda de sa Punta

Cala'n Bruch

Cala'n Blanes

Beach

Carretera de Ciutadella a Cala'n Blanes

Rent a Bike ✳✳

Velosplay hire family-sized bikes (for four, five or six people) by the hour – a fun way to explore the resorts. *Avinguda de los Delfines. Open 0900–2100.*

BEACHES

Each of the four coves has its own separate beach. The beach at Cala'n Blanes is long and sandy, with sunbeds, parasols and pedalos for hire and shady pinewoods behind the sand. Cala'n Bruch has very little sand, but the concrete platforms above the long, narrow creek are perfect for sunbathing or for diving into the clear water. Cala'n Forcat has a wide, sandy beach at the edge of a tiny cove, while Cales Piques has a small beach reached by a flight of steps.

RESTAURANTS AND BARS *(see map on pages 68–69)*

El Abuelo £ ❶ Everyone's welcome at 'the grandfather', where the good value menu features *paella*, grilled chicken and a mixed seafood grill. *Avinguda de los Delfines. Tel: 971 388154. Open 0930–2300.*

L'Ancora £ ❷ This popular restaurant serves barbecued meat and fish on a shady garden terrace. *Avinguda Simón de Olivar, Cala'n Blanes. Tel: 971 388405. Open 0900–midnight.*

Churchill's Bar £ ❸ Good place to sit back and relax. Bouncy castle and pool tables for children. *Calas Picas 225, 4–5, Cala'n Blanes, Citudella. Tel: 971 388754. Open 1000–0200.*

Sr. Donald's £ ❹ Fish 'n' chip shop with tables on the terrace. *Tel: 971 388014. Calas Picas 225, 2, Cala'n Blanes, Citudella. Open 1000–1400 & 1830–2330.*

Cala'n Bruch £ ❺ Creekside snack bar with a relaxed family atmosphere and wonderful sea views. The specialities include beef stroganoff and vegetarian lasagne. *Avinguda Cala'n Bruch. Open 1000–2300.*

Ca'n Moll £ ❻ Menorcan fish dishes, such as grilled hake, rabbit in almond sauce and chicken with prawns, as well as a wide range of pizzas, served on a garden terrace. *Avinguda Simón de Olivar, Cala'n Blanes. Tel: 971 388490. Open 1000–midnight.*

Mangiare Felici at Ses Truqueries £££ ❼ Italian and international cuisine in a country house setting. Very special. On the road to Ciutadella. *On the road to Ciutadella. Tel: 971 359159. Open 1300–1530 and from 2000, except Mon lunchtime.*

Indiana Bill £ ❽ Menorca's answer to KFC, with an adjoining children's play area. *Carrer d'Escorel. Tel: 609 763026. Open 1000–midnight.*

Lynne's Little Chippy £ ❾ Typical English-style fish'n'chips, made with English potatoes and English fish. *Carrer Simon de Oliver 117. Tel: 616 707820. Open 1200–1400 & 1800–2300.*

El Patio ££ ❿ Seafood restaurant specialising in fish (especially lobster casserole), with marvellous views out to sea. *Avinguda de los Delfines. Tel: 919 184864. Open 1200–1530 & 1830–2300.*

Sa Caldereta ££ ⓫ Menorcan classics, such as lobster stew and roast shoulder of lamb, in a friendly family restaurant with a separate children's menu. *Avinguda de los Delfines. Tel: 971 388212. Open 1100–midnight.*

NIGHTLIFE

Blue Breeze ⓬ Friendly, modern cocktail bar with pool tables, ice-hockey game and a happy hour 2300–midnight. *Cales Piques. Tel: 971 388153. Open 1500–0400.*

Cheers ⓭ This lively bar has karaoke until midnight followed by disco music till 0400. Happy hour 2300–midnight. *Cales Piques. Open 2100–0400.*

Danzas ⓮ Disco at the heart of the Los Delfines complex. Free entry for families until midnight; adults only after this. *Avinguda de los Delfines. Open 2000 till late.*

Green Parrot ⓯ Lots of fun and frolics at this English-run bar. Happy hour 2100–2200. *Carrer des Canal, Cala'n Bruch. Open 1900–0400 (disco from midnight).*

Cala'n Bruch

Fornells – peaceful fishing village

With its low whitewashed cottages, fishing boats bobbing in the breeze, and stately palm trees guarding a seafront promenade, Fornells is everyone's idea of a Mediterranean fishing village. The fishermen still set out from Fornells each morning to catch the spiny lobsters which are the ingredient at the heart of Menorca's most famous dish – caldereta de langosta, or lobster casserole.

Fornells has its own beach resort – Playa de Fornells – 2 miles (3.2km) out of town in the bay of Cala Tirant. The villas here are built in local style and many of them have attractive gardens bursting with different varieties of cactus plants. Between here and the village is the watersports centre of Ses Salines. But most visitors head straight for the village itself. Built on the west side of the Bay of Fornells, with its calm waters and long natural harbour, Fornells was originally founded to defend the north coast against pirate ships. Follow the waterfront beyond the fish restaurants around the main square and you come to the ruins of a 17th-century fortress, Castell Sant Antoni. Keep going and you soon reach the headland, buffeted by wind and waves, where a tiny chapel is built into the rock and you can walk right inside a restored watch-tower and imagine yourself on sentry duty looking out for enemy ships.

What brings people to Fornells today is the chance to try the celebrated *caldereta*. The ingredients are simple: a lobster, some tomatoes and onions, a bit of garlic and parsley. Cook it all in an earthenware bowl and serve with wafers of dry bread to dip into the soup and a set of tools for prising the lobster apart. All the restaurants in Fornells serve it – yet each one is different and each chef jealously guards his own recipe. It is certainly expensive, but an experience to remember – King Juan Carlos of Spain regularly sails his yacht over from his Mallorcan holiday home to eat *caldereta de langosta* at his favourite restaurant, Es Pla. How often do you get the chance to eat like a king?

THINGS TO SEE AND DO

Scuba diving *
Scuba-diving courses are offered at the Diving Centre, Fornells. *Passeig Maritim 44B. Tel: 971 376431.*

Watersports **
The Bay of Fornells is ideal for novice sailors and windsurfers because of its calm waters and gentle breezes. Windsurf Fornells, at the entrance to the village, has dinghies, catamarans and windsurfing equipment for hire and can offer lessons for beginners and more advanced sailors. There is also water-skiing available here. *Tel: 971 376400.*

EXCURSIONS

Cap de Cavallería **
From Fornells you can follow a bumpy road to Menorca's northernmost point, the lighthouse at Cap de Cavallería, where wild goats graze on rocky headlands lashed by wind and waves. Along the way you pass the old Roman port of Sanitja, now a pretty harbour, with tracks leading to the unspoiled beaches of Cavallería and Farragut.

BEACHES

Playa de Fornells has its own small beach, with a footpath leading around the bay to the larger beach at Cala Tirant, where a beach bar rents out sunbeds, umbrellas and pedalos. Fornells is a good starting point for excursions to some of the wilder north coast beaches, especially Binimel-là and its neighbour Cala Pregonda, which can only be reached on foot.

RESTAURANTS AND BARS

Cranc Palut ££ Quiet, out-of-the-way restaurant serving *paella*, meat dishes and fried squid, overlooking the bay at the end of the seafront promenade. *Passeig Maritim 98. Tel: 971 376743. Open 1300–1630, 2000–midnight. Closed Tues.*

Es Cranc ££ Where the locals come to eat *caldereta de langosta* – no outdoor chairs and no sea views, just tremendous home cooking and a very Spanish atmosphere. *Carrer Escoles 31. Tel: 971 376442. Open 1330–1600 & 2000–midnight. Closed Wed.*

La Palma/S'Algaret £ These two *tapas* bars on the main square are always bustling with locals and visitors. *Plaza S'Algaret 3 & 7. Tel: 971 376634 (la Palma) or 971 376666 (S'Algaret). Both open 0800–midnight.*

Es Passeig Marítim ££ This is better value than many of the waterfront restaurants – everything from pizzas and *paella* to a gourmet menu featuring octopus, mussels and lobster. *Passeig Marítim 45. Tel: 971 376312. Open 1200–1500 & 1900–midnight.*

El Pescador £££ Wicker chairs on the waterfront and a wide variety of fish and seafood dishes – try the hot red peppers stuffed with prawns. *Carrer de S'Algaret 3. Tel: 971 376538. Open 1200–midnight.*

Es Pla £££ Imagine you're a king as you eat lobster at the water's edge. Some lower mortals consider this restaurant rather too formal. *Avinguda Poeta Gumersindo Riera. Tel: 971 376655. Open 1300–1500 & 2000–2230.*

Es Port ££ Lobster casserole, and grilled meat and fish, are the specialities at this friendly waterfront restaurant. *Tel: 971 376403. Avinguda Poeta Gumersindo Riera 5. Tel: 971 376403. Open 1200–1600 & 1900–2300.*

Rosa Negra £ Hilltop snack bar overlooking the beach at Playa de Fornells. *Tel: 971 376716. Open 1300–0300. Closed Mon lunch.*

S'Ancora ££ Popular fish restaurant directly facing the harbour. One of the set menus features a small tasting of *caldereta de langosta* at an affordable price. *Avinguda Poeta Gumersindo Riera 7 & 8. Tel: 971 376670. Open 1200–1500 & 1930–2300.*

TIP! If you don't want to spend a fortune, try *caldereta de mariscos* – this seafood and fish casserole is the same dish without the lobster, and you may even get a lobster claw thrown in.

Arenal d'en Castell and Son Parc –
relaxing beach resorts

The north-east coast between Fornells and Maó is the setting for two of Menorca's biggest and best beaches, as well as a string of smaller bays and coves. The coastline here is backed by sand dunes, with acres of thick pine forest inland. The two big resorts have plenty of restaurants and nightlife, but much of this area is quiet and unspoiled.

The beach at Arenal d'en Castell is perfect – an oyster-shaped bay of fine sand, protected from the harsh east wind by the headland of Punta Grossa. Children can swim safely in the shallow water and facilities range from beach bars to windsurfing. Nearby Addaia is a peaceful and beautiful resort, set around a yacht marina at the entrance to a long, sheltered creek.

From Arenal d'en Castell you can walk along the coast to Son Parc, another fine beach resort containing Menorca's only golf course. Sa Roca, a few miles inland, is a real get-away-from-it-all destination – nothing more than a few villas in the middle of pinewoods, in the shadow of Menorca's highest mountain, Monte Toro.

 TIP! Don't forget to keep an eye on the safety flags while swimming at Arenal d'en Castell – a green flag means it is safe to swim, yellow means take care, and red means don't swim at all.

THINGS TO SEE AND DO

Club Son Parc Golf *
Visitors are welcome to use this nine-hole course (by reservation), along with the driving range, putting green and tennis courts. Club hire is available, but golfers are asked not to come in their beach gear! *On the road into Son Parc. Tel: 971 188875. Web: www.clubsonparc.com.*

Watersports *

Both Son Parc and Arenal d'en Castell have facilities for windsurfing, while
sailing dinghies can be hired from the marina in Addaia. Addaia also has the
Ulmo Diving Centre, with tuition for beginners and more advanced sub-aqua
divers. *Tel: 971 188996. Open Mon–Sat 0900–1930, Sun 0900–1400.*

Hort de Llucaitx Park ***

Excellent facilities are available to dine (at the restaurant or BBQ), to hire horses
and ponies, and to entertain children at the playground or the animal farm.
*Carretera Maó-Fornells km 17 (near Son Parc turn-off). Tel: 629 392894. Open
all year from 1000–1900. Bar open all day; restaurant at weekends only.*

BEACHES

The beaches at Arenal d'en Castell and Son Parc have all the facilities you would
expect and are big enough to cope with large numbers of sun-worshippers.
Both have shallow water and are suitable for families. A 20-minute walk from
Son Parc, crossing a herb-scented headland from behind the beach bar, leads
to the pretty cove of Cala Pudent, where the beach is usually deserted. There
is no beach at Addaia, but the nearby village of Na Macaret has a small beach
and several good restaurants at the water's edge.

RESTAURANTS AND BARS

 **Alcalde ££** Classic Menorcan dishes, such as roast kid, fish stew
and steak with Mahón cheese sauce, overlooking the beach at
Arenal d'en Castell. *Carrer Romani, Arenal d'en Castell. Tel: 971 358093.
Open 1100–2300.*

 **El Mirador £** Pizzas and *paella* high above the beach at Arenal
d'en Castell, with wonderful views from the shaded terrace and a
swimming pool. *Carrer Estrella. Tel: 971 358130. Open 1000–0300 (pool
open 1000–1900).*

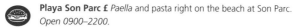 **Playa Son Parc £** *Paella* and pasta right on the beach at Son Parc.
Open 0900–2200.

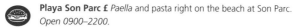 **Las Plumas £££** The restaurant in the golf clubhouse at Son Parc
has a new English chef offering high-class international cuisine.
*Tel: 971 188875. Open 1200–1600 & 1930–midnight. The bar is open
0900–midnight.*

Puig de Sa Roca £££ A special place for a celebration meal – a restaurant and swimming pool deep in the pine woods, serving traditional Spanish cuisine on a large terrace. Try the roast suckling pig or the cod with sultanas and spinach. Booking advised. *Sa Roca. Tel: 971 188642. Open 1200–1600, 2000–midnight.*

Restaurante Addaia ££ *Flambés* are the house special at this popular Spanish restaurant. How about prawns flamed in whisky or lobster flamed in *calvados*? *Zona Comercial, Addaia. Tel: 971 359261. Open 1100–1600 & 1800–2330.*

Rex's Pub £ Homesick Brits gather at this typical English pub for hearty cooked breakfasts and roast dinners. *Plaça Comercial, Son Parc. Tel: 971 359105. Open 0900–0030.*

S'Arenal ££ This restaurant and pizzeria right on the beach at Arenal d'en Castell has live music every night. The house speciality is chicken, *flambéd* in a green peppercorn sauce. *Tel: 971 636592. Open 1930–2330.*

Sagitario £ Very child-friendly, with a play area and a children's menu featuring 14 dishes. Adults can choose between risotto, pizza, curry and steak. *Plaça Comercial, Son Parc. Tel: 971 359025. Open 1300–2300.*

Tots Pub £ *Tapas* bar which is popular with the locals, including the large British community in Son Parc. Typical snacks include mussels, squid, crab and snails. *Son Parc. Open 1830–0300.*

Venecia £ Italian pizzeria and pasta bar overlooking the bay. The Japi bar attached to the restaurant attracts a young crowd at night. *Carrer Romani, Arenal d'en Castell. Tel: 971 358247. Open 1100–midnight.*

NIGHTLIFE

The Corner Bar This Irish pub is the in place to meet in Addaia. Regular live entertainment and a large selection of Irish whiskeys. *Zona Comercial. Open 1900 till late (karaoke Sun 2100–0100).*

Av. de la Verge del Toro

C de Ciutadella

Es Porrassar Vell

Caminet des Pou Nou

Carrer de l'Angel

Avinguda de la Verge del Toro

Menorca

Mallorca

Església
Santa Eulàlia ❶

Costa des Pou

Carrer de les Escoles

Carrer de s'Arraval

Carrer de Baixamar

Costa de l'Església

Carrer Major

Santa Rita

Town Hall

❸

Carrer Nou

❹

Claustre
Sant Diego

Sports
Cenrte

Del Mestre
Duran

🚌

Joan Baptista de la Salle

Carrer des Ramal

Sant Josep

Carrer des Banyer

Carrer de Balmes

Carrer de Miguel de Cervantes

Carrer des
Comerç

Avinguda del Pare Huguet

Carrer de sa Bassa Roja

Carrer des Mellang

Carretera Nova

Carrer de
Ruiz I Pablo

Carretera Nova

❷

Ciutadella - Mahon

Alaior –
Menorca's 'third capital'

Alaior (pronounced 'Allay-*or*') is sometimes referred to as Menorca's 'third capital', due to its historical role as a mediator between Maó and Ciutadella, and also because of the wealth and independence afforded it by its thriving leather and cheese industries.

Tourism has largely ignored the town and few visitors actually take the time to stop and explore the cool, shaded streets of Alaior, draped over a hill just off the main Maó to Ciutadella road. Those who do are richly rewarded by the striking architecture of many of its fine townhouses, the ornate Town Hall and the vast church of Santa Eulàlia. Be sure also to see the handicraft markets, the splendid views of the surrounding countryside from the water-tower at the top of the town and the striking church of San Diego, whose ancient cloisters have been converted into modern flats and whose courtyard, known as Sa Lluna, is a popular summer setting for concerts and folk-dancing.

Alaior's main claim to fame, however, is that it is the home of Admiral Nelson's favourite cheese, the island's renowned Mahón cheese, originally named after the port (Maó, also called Mahón) where it was first made and exported. Today, it is still made in the traditional way in Alaior, from recipes passed down from generation to generation. You can buy it in various stages of maturity from *fresco* (fresh and soft) to *anejo* (matured for two years, and as strong as Parmesan). The more mature types travel well and make good presents.

 August is the best time to visit Alaior, to see the popular fiesta of Sant Llorenç, flamboyant celebrations known in particular for their showy horse parades. Check with your holiday representative or at Maó's Tourist Office for exact dates.

BEACHES

The largest beach on the island is just 5 miles' (8km) drive away, at Son Bou (*see page 49*).

THINGS TO SEE AND DO

Picadero Menorca *

This popular ranch on the outskirts of Alaior offers pony treks, rides in a horse and cart, and special lessons for children. *Carretera Alaior–Son Bou (just off the roundabout beneath the C721). Tel: 608 323566.*

Prehistoric treasures **

The wealth of prehistoric remains near Alaior are well worth exploring, notably:

● **Torralba d'en Salort**, which boasts the island's most magnificent T-shaped stone structure called a *taula*. *Carretera Alaior–Cala'n Porter. Open 1000–1400 & 1600–2000.*

● **Sa Torre d'en Gaumes**, the largest prehistoric settlement on the island. *Carretera Alaior–Son Bou.*

● **Cales Coves** necropolis (*see page 43*), an extraordinary honeycomb of ancient burial caves gouged out of a cliff face.

EXCURSION

Camí d'en Kane **

Menorca's first British governor, Sir Richard Kane, built a road across the island from Maó to Ciutadella – paid for by a tax on alcohol. The first section of the road (from Maó to Alaior) has recently been repaired and a drive along 'Kane's road' is a good way of experiencing the typical Menorcan countryside of cattle and flower-filled meadows. *Turn left off the main road to Maó, following signs for the Camí d'en Kane.*

Alaior's narrow streets

SHOPPING

Markets There is a craft market in front of the church of Santa Eulàlia every Saturday morning, and a weekly produce market on Thursdays in Avinguda del Pare Huguet.

For cheese, try the factory shops of **La Payesa** down an unlikely-looking back street at *Carrer d'es Banyer 64. Open Mon–Fri 0900–1300 & 1600–1900, closed Sat.* Or what about **Coinga** in the Industrial Estate on the edge of town? *Carrer d'es Mercadal. Open Mon–Fri 0900–1300 & 1630–2030, Sat 0900–1330.*

The main shopping street Carrer des Ramal has a selection of tempting stores including **Calzados Alaior** at no 19 for shoes, **Blanc i Verd** at no 16 with its fine jewellery, pottery, wood and canvas gifts.

RESTAURANTS AND BARS *(see map on page 82)*

The Cobblers £££ ❶ One of the best restaurants on the island, in an elegant townhouse, once the home of a famous local shoemaker, hence the name. Most of the year, dinner is served in the delightful courtyard. *Carrer San Macario 6. Tel: 971 371400. Open Mon–Sat 1900–2300. Closed Sun. Advance booking recommended.*

Es Plans ££ ❷ Feeling homesick? Come here for fish'n'chips with mushy peas, steak-and-kidney pie – even a full roast dinner on Sundays! *Carretera Maó–Ciutadella, km 14, 8. Tel: 971 378038. Open Tues–Sun 1900–2300 & Sun 1230–1500. Closed Mon.*

Transparent £ ❸ This trendy café bar in a spacious square is popular with locals and visitors alike. There's a playground opposite to keep children amused. *Plaça Ramal 22. Tel: 971 372796. Open 1100–0200.*

Ximenes ££ ❹ It's easy to miss the entrance to this basement restaurant. Once you find it, you'll be rewarded with hearty island cuisine. The two-course *menú del día* at lunchtimes is especially good value. *Carrer des Forn 2. Tel: 971 371120. Open 1300–1500 & 1930–2200. Closed Sun evening.*

Opposite: One of Alaior's characterful courtyards

Es Mercadal –
Mediterranean market town

The picturesque old market town of Es Mercadal
(pronounced 'Es Merk-a-*dal*'), at the geographical
centre of the island, is known for its traditional
crafts, its gastronomy, and the flamboyant displays
of horsemanship during its dazzling July fiesta.

The name 'Mercadal' originates from the fact that the town was once
the major market town of the island, where locals came to sell their fruit,
vegetables and traditional wares, and to this day there remains a handicraft
market, held on Tuesday and Saturday afternoons. Besides farming, the main
industries here are the production of *abarcas* (sandals with soles made out
of tyres), confectionery and almond macaroons.

THINGS TO SEE AND DO

Explore the old town *
As well as shopping on the main street (Carrer Nou), and lapping up the local
colour of the busy main square (Plaça Constitució), be sure to explore the
sleepy historic part of town, where whitewashed cottages straddle an ancient
reservoir built on the orders of the first British governor, Sir Richard Kane.

Monte Toro ***
Es Mercadal is also the starting point for the ascent of Monte Toro, Menorca's
highest mountain, named after a *toro* (wild bull) who, many years ago, led
a party of nuns to a hidden cave containing a statue of the Madonna and
Child. The convent at the top has been a place of pilgrimage ever since and
is still inhabited by nuns. There is also a gift shop and café. Despite the forest
of aerials and radar dishes, the views from the terrace are sensational. Most
days, you can see the entire island and, if the visibility is especially good, it
is sometimes possible to see Mallorca. For the best photo opportunities, aim
to be at the top just before sunset.

Sa Farinera **
The museum of the old flour mill, on the main road just outside Mercadal,
comes complete with a commercial area (*open 1000–2100*), a children's
playground and a restaurant (*open 1100–0100*).

 TIP! Keep children amused in the car on the main road from Es Mercadal to Maó trying to spot a gigantic rock near the roadside shaped like the head of an Indian chief, known as Sa Penya Cabeza del Indio (Indian Head Peak). As you head towards Maó, it's on the right-hand side of the road (opposite a small lay-by) between Es Mercadal and Alaior.

BEACHES

Two of Menorca's finest beaches lie within easy reach of Es Mercadal on the north coast – Binimel-là with its striking red sand and pebbles, backed by sand dunes, and Cala Pregonda, with its deserted sandy beach and crystal-clear waters, a 30-minute walk along the coast from Binimel-là.

RESTAURANTS AND BARS

Ca'n Aguedet £££ Exquisite Menorcan cuisine and a good list of local wines. Try the snails with mayonnaise, then rabbit with figs, followed by a moreish dessert. The pinenut and raisin cake is particularly delicious. *Carrer Lepanto 23. Tel: 971 375391. Open 1300–1600 & 2000–2330.*

Ca'n Olga ££ Dine alfresco in a pretty garden, hidden down an alleyway in the old part of town. The cooking is Mediterranean style, and the *menú del día* is especially good value. *Pont de Na Macarrana, Carrer d'es Sol. Tel: 971 375459. Open 2000–2330.*

Ets Arcs ££ Don't be put off by the exterior as there is a charming terrace at the back where you can enjoy generous portions of rabbit with garlic, onions stuffed with seafood and other local dishes. *Carretera Maó–Ciutadella. Tel: 971 375538. Open 1300–1600 & 1900–2300.*

Jeni ££ A modern bar serving mouth-watering steaks, stuffed peppers and seafood. *Carrer Mirada del Toro 81. Tel: 971 375059. Open 0700–0030.*

Molí d'es Racó ££ An atmospheric restaurant, housed in an old windmill, serving traditional Menorcan specialities. *Carrer Vicario Fuxà 53. Tel: 971 375392. Open 1300–1600 & 1900–2300.*

Sa Plaça £ A no-frills locals' bar in the main square, especially popular for morning coffee and *tapas* snacks. *Plaça Constitucio 2. Tel: 971 375048. Open 0700–2330.*

SHOPPING

Ca'n Pons This small, rather ordinary-looking bakery sells the best almond macaroons on the island. *Carrer Nou 13. Tel: 971 375175. Open 0930–1330 & 1700–2030.*

Ca's Sucrer An old-fashioned sweet shop, with jars of sweets neatly arranged on shelves around the store – an absolute must for those with a sweet tooth! *Plaça Constitucio 11. Tel: 971 375175. Open 0930–1330 & 1630–2000.*

Galeria del Sol Affordable pottery and paintings of Menorca by local artists. *Carrer d'es Sol. Tel: 971 375125. Open Mon–Sat 1000–1400 & 1900–2200. Closed Sun.*

Casa Servera Traditional *abarcas* (sandals) made on the premises. *Avinguda Metge Camps 3. Tel: 971 375384. Open 0900–1330 & 1700–2030. Closed Sun.*

Carrer de Goya

Carretera General

Glorieta dels Martirs

Plaça del Princep D. Juan Carlos ⑤

Plaça de la Constitocio

Carrer de son Granot

Carrer d'es Torrenter

Carrer Fred

C. Mestre Obrador

Carrer de sa Pau

Carrer de Rvnd Guillem Coll

Avda de son Morera

C. Ecònom Florit ②

Avinguda de la Verge del Toro

Carrer del Bisbe Sever

① ③

Costa de ses Barreres

Plaça Espanya ■ Market

Carrer del Rvnd J Huguet

C/ de sa Sinia

Plaça de L'Esglesia

✉ San Bartomen

Carrer Pau Pons

Town Hall ■

Carrer Sant Bartomeu

Carrer del Dega

C/ de Ciutadella

Plaça Francesc D'Albranca

Carrer de sa Font

Carrer Eivissa

Carrer Mallorca ④

Carrer Formentera

Doctor Febrer

Plaça Menorca

■ Museu de la Natura

Carretera Pm 713

Carrer d'es Migjorn Gran

Carrer de l'epanto

Torrent de Son Granot

N

0　　　100　　　200 m

Ferreries –
Menorca's highest town

Bustling Ferreries (pronounced 'Ferrer-*ree*-es') was once totally dependent on agriculture and dairy farming. Nowadays, it has expanded and enjoys a thriving industry of shoe making, jewellery and furniture and is a popular shopping stop en route from Maó to Ciutadella.

The name of the town (from *ferreria*, the Catalan word for 'blacksmith') derives from its early reputation for making iron door hinges. The highest town on the island, it is also at the heart of Menorca's most fertile zone, and every Saturday morning there is a small market in Plaça Espanya where farmers from the surrounding area offer their produce of fruits, vegetables, cheeses, biscuits, honey, herbs and handicrafts.

Near by, the main square – Plaça de l'Esglesia – is one of the prettiest corners of town flanked by the small church of San Bartomeu, and the town hall with its brightly coloured flags. The narrow jumble of sun-baked back streets with their neatly shuttered, whitewashed houses has an air of typical Mediterranean tranquillity.

 The shopping complex at Castillo Menorca near Ferreries is a great port of call for all the family – an excellent range of souvenir shops for those who love them and a bar and newspaper shop for those who don't! *Carretera Maó–Ciutadella, km 35. Tel: 971 380424.* There is also the Lladró shop with one of the largest collections of porcelain figurines in Europe.

BEACHES
From Ferreries by car, you can easily reach the beautiful beaches of Sant Tomás, Binigaus (*see page 54*), Cala Mitjana and Cala Galdana (*see page 58*).

THINGS TO SEE AND DO

Costa Nova Karting Club *
Children of all ages love whizzing around the go-kart tracks here. *Carretera Maó–Ciutadella, km 35. Tel: 971 380424. Open 1000–2000. Admission charge.*

Espectacle Ecuestre de Menorca **
Marvel at the equestrian skills of the Club Escola Menorquina riding stables, at their twice-weekly demonstrations of typically Menorcan dressage skills, including the prancing and controlled rearing often seen at island fiestas. During the interval, there are donkey rides for the children. *Carretera Cala Galdana, km 0.5. Tel: 971 155059. Shows June–Sept, Wed & Sun 2030. There are also shows 1 km further on the same road on Tues and Thurs at 2030.*

Museu de la Natura *
A fascinating, new and interactive museum, which brings to life the history, culture and nature of the island. *Carrer Mallorca 2. Tel: 971 350762. Open May–Sept Tues–Sun 1000–1300 & 1800–2100, Oct–Apr Tues–Sun 1000–2100, Sat 1000–1300 & 1800–2100. Admission charge.*

EXCURSIONS

Binisues *
This beautiful country manor provides a fascinating insight into aristocratic life here in bygone days. There is also a first-class restaurant (*see page 96*) with magnificent views of central Menorca. *Carretera Maó–Ciutadella, km 31, 6, then the turn-off to the right (signposted to Binisues). Tel: 971 373728. Open 1100–1900. Closed Mon. Admission charge.*

Castell Santa Agueda *
The hour-long hike to the top of Mount Santa Agueda, one of Menorca's highest hills, is well worth the effort, not so much for the ruined Moorish fort at the top, but for the breathtaking island vistas and for the incredible sense of history along the original Roman road that forms a section of the walk. To find the start of the walk, continue up the same road as for Binisues and, just before the tarmac stops, there is a clearing on the right-hand side to leave your car, and wooden signs indicating the route.

Ferreries market

RESTAURANTS AND BARS (see map on page 92)

Binisues £££ ❶ A top-notch restaurant offering a wide range of meat and fish dishes. The proprietor has his own fishing boats and lobster pots at Ciutadella, so the house specialities include the freshest of fish, shellfish and lobster casserole. *Just off Carretera Maó–Ciutadella, at km 31, 6. Tel: 971 373728. Open Tues–Sun 1200–1630 & 1900–2330. Closed Mon.*

Liorna ££ ❷ This gem of a restaurant is hidden down a back street in the older part of town. Ask for a table in the garden. *Carrer Econom Florit 9. Tel: 971 373912. Open 1900–2300.*

Mesón El Gallo ££ ❸ Try one of the specialities – parrillada (mixed barbecue grill), steak with Mahón cheese or *paella de Gallo* at this 200-year-old farmhouse restaurant. *Carretera Cala Santa Galdana, km 1.5. Tel: 971 373039. Open Tues–Sun 1330–1500 & 1930–2300. Closed Mon.*

Mesón Galicia £ ❹ A small, homely restaurant and *tapas* bar serving hearty meat and fish dishes from Galicia, in northern Spain. *Carretera Maó 15. Tel: 971 373883. Open Thurs–Sun only.*

Vimpi £ ❺ This no-frills locals' bar serves some of the best *tapas* on the island. Try stuffed mushrooms, squid and local cured ham. *Plaça Joan Carles 5. Tel: 971 373199. Open 0600–midnight.*

SHOPPING

Shoes are a good buy in Ferreries. Try the huge **Jaime Mascaro** factory outlet, the **Ferrerias Centre** and **Industrial Artesanas Menorca** factory shop on the industrial estate on the outskirts of town.

Artesania Maria Janer You are sure to find some unusual presents from the large choice of quality pottery, wood, glass and paper gifts here. *Carrer Font 24. Tel: 971 374002.*

Los Claveles This specialist bakery produces Menorcan biscuits and pastries. *Avinguda Verge del Monte Toro 4. Tel: 971 373128.*

Noveta d'es Tudons

Camí de Maó

Camí de Maó

Av. de Jaume I El Conqueridor

C. de Mossen L. S. i Farrés

Praça d'Alfons III

Avinguda de la Constitució

Praça Nova

Praça d'Alfruix

Av. Capita Negrete

C. Sta. Clara

C. 3ª i Nº Quadrado (es Voltes)

C. Sr. Sébastia

Cathedral

Praça de la Catedral

C. de la Purissima

C. de Sa Muradella

Praça de's Born

Praça dels Pins

Es Pla de Sant Joan

Museu del Pintor Torrent

Port de Ciudadella

Carrer de la Marina

Avinguda Gabriel Roca

Boats trips

Passeig de Sant Nicolau

Camí de Baix

Boats for Mallorca

Ciutadella –
Menorca's ancient capital

Nowhere else in Menorca feels quite so Spanish as Ciutadella (pronounced '*Suit*-a-della') – also sometimes called Ciudadela, or 'little city'. When the British moved the capital to Maó, the bishop and noble families stayed behind, and their palaces can still be seen today. The Plaça d'es Born, the old parade ground at the heart of the city, is one of the finest squares in Spain.

In Ciutadella it is a pleasure just to stroll the narrow streets of the old town, located between 'the Born' and the Plaça de Ses Palmeres ('Palm Tree Square'). Wander down any of these streets and you can peer into the courtyards of old mansions – with their balconies, stone archways and coats of arms above the doors. Artists and jewellers have set up their workshops in the back streets near the cathedral, among the up-market boutiques selling designer clothes. Come here in the early evening, as the people of Ciutadella gather beneath the whitewashed arches of Ses Voltes or stop for a drink at the bars in Plaça Nova, and you can really get the feel of this fascinating city.

 Watch the sun go down behind the Castell de Sant Nicolau, an old watch-tower on the waterfront half-way along the Passeig Marítim. The views of Mallorca, as it turns pink on the horizon, are magical.

THINGS TO SEE AND DO

Cathedral **
Menorca's Gothic cathedral was built on the site of a former mosque and the old minaret has been turned into a belfry. *Open 0800–1300 & 1800–2100.*

Cruise the coast **

Take a day trip by boat from Ciutadella harbour to some of the island's most beautiful beaches, Cala Son Saura, Cala'n Turqueta and Cala Macarella. Most companies include free *paella* and *sangría* in the price.

Hire a bike *

A great way to explore the city and the surrounding countryside! *Bicicletas Tolo, Carrer Sant Isidre 28. Tel: 971 381576. Open Mon–Fri 0800–1300 & 1530–1930, Sat 0900–1300, Sun 1830–1930.*

Museu del Pintor Torrent *

Art lovers will enjoy this small, permanent exhibition of work by the late Pintor Torrent, the 'Van Gogh of Menorca'. *Carrer Sant Rafael 11. Open 1100–1300 & 1930–2130.*

Naveta d'es Tudons **

This Bronze Age burial chamber in the shape of an upturned boat was restored to its original condition in 1975. You can crawl right inside on your hands and knees. *On the main road from Ciutadella to Maó, 2^1/2 miles (4km) from Ciutadella.*

Carrer de Marina ***

This seafront promenade, opened in 1997, is where the locals come to join in the sunset ritual of the *paseo*, or evening stroll. The full walk, from the Plaça d'es Born to the small beach at Cala d'es Degollador, takes a leisurely half an hour each way and the views along the seafront are superb.

Plaça d'es Born ***

The Born is the meeting place of Ciutadella and it is great fun to sit outside one of the pavement cafés watching the world go by. From the old city walls on the north side there is a good view of the fishing harbour at the end of a long, narrow creek.

Ciutadella, Menorca's former capital

A perfect end to the day

BEACHES

Ciutadella's beach is at Cala d'es Degollador, a short walk from the centre at the end of the Carrer de Marina. Most people head for the larger beaches at Sa Caleta and Cala Santandria (*see page 64*), or the rocky coves to the north of the city.

EXCURSIONS

Cala Morell **

Just 5 miles (8km) away on the largely deserted north-east coast of the island, this small, exclusive resort is best known for the prehistoric caves in the cliffs, which frame a picturesque cove and pocket-handkerchief-sized beach. The swimming and snorkelling is excellent here, just as it is at the idyllic, sandy beaches of Algaiarens near by.

Mallorca **

Mallorca is just 75 minutes away from Ciutadella by fast boat (organised by Cape Balear sailing company). Daily sailings 0730 from Ciutadella return 2100 from Cala Ratjada, Mallorca. *Moll Comercial. Tel: 971 818668.*

RESTAURANTS AND BARS *(see map on page 98)*

 Bar Ulises £ ❶ Join locals here for an early morning coffee in the market square. *Plaça de la Llibertat. Tel: 971 380031. Open Mon–Fri 0630–1500 & 1830–2100 (Fri 2300), Sat 0630–1500. Closed Sun.*

SHOPPING

The Old Town The narrow streets of the old quarter are full of small, specialist shops. Try Carrer Seminari for art, jewellery and antiques, Carrer de Sa Carnisseria for clothes, and the central street, usually known as Ses Voltes, for just about anything. Two good shoe shops in Ses Voltes are Looky and Ca Sa Pollaca, which has been selling handmade leather shoes since 1897. Ses Industries, in Carrer Santa Clara, has a good selection of Spanish wines and spirits.

The colourful **daily market** in Plaça de la Llibertat is a fun place to shop for fish and foodstuffs.

The Magic House This toy shop promises hours of fun for children of all ages. *Carrer Major del Borne 7. Tel: 971 385040. Open Mon–Sat 1000–2130. Closed Sun.*

Sa Gelateria de Menorca This ice-cream company is famous throughout Spain and offers a dazzling choice of flavours. The orange and yoghurt ice is especially refreshing. *Costa d'es Moll. Open 1100– 0100. Closed Sun 1200–1400.*

Hiper Ciutadella Out-of-town hypermarket on the road to Cala'n Bosch. *Open Mon–Sat 0900–2100.*

 Café Central £ ❷ A popular *tapas* bar right beside the cathedral. *Plaça Catedral. Tel: 971 482208. Open 0900–2300.*

 C'as Quinto £ ❸ This *tapas* bar, specialising in seafood, is a Ciutadella institution. You can sit out of doors beneath the palm trees, enjoying grilled prawns, fried squid rings or the mussels known as 'sea dates'. *Avinguda de la Constitució 17, Citudella. Tel: 971381 002. Open 0900–0100.*

 Casa Manolo £££ ❹ The best of the many seafood restaurants lining Ciutadella's harbour. The lobster casserole is expensive, but out of this world. *Carrer de Marina 117. Tel: 971 380003. Open 1300–1600 & 2000–2300.*

Don Giacomo ££ ❺ Pizzas from a wood-fired oven, and imaginative Mediterranean dishes, such as duck with pears, served in an old townhouse close to the main square. *Carrer Nou de Juliol 5. Tel: 971 383279. Open 1100–1600 & 1900–0100.*

La Guitarra ££ ❻ Classic Menorcan cuisine at very reasonable prices in a basement cellar in the old town. *Carrer Nostra Senyora dels Dolors 1. Tel: 971 381355. Open 1200–1530 & 1900–2300. Closed Sun.*

El Horno ££ ❼ A sophisticated French restaurant. Try the rabbit with red wine and mushrooms, or chicken in cream and tarragon sauce. *Carrer d'es Forn. Tel: 971 380767. Open 1900–2200.*

Es Moll £ ❽ This simple Menorcan restaurant by the harbour is perfectly placed to catch the lunchtime sun and its daily lunchtime menu is excellent value. *Moll Comercial. Tel: 971 480813. Open 1030–1530 & 1900–midnight.*

Marieta £ ❾ This open-air waterfront café is always a hive of activity, and serves delicious sandwiches, salads and pancakes day and night. *Carrer de Marina. Open Mon–Sat 1000–0400, Sun 1900–0400.*

Pa Amb Oli £ ❿ The place to try *pa amb oli* (*see Tapas on page 108*), with baskets of garlic and tomatoes on the tables to rub on your toast. The other speciality is charcoal-grilled meat and vegetables. *Carrer Nou de Juliol. Tel: 971 480489. Open 0800–midnight.*

NIGHTLIFE

Aladino ⓫ A trendy harbourside cocktail bar and dance club. *Carrer de Marina. Open 1930–0400.*

Asere ⓬ Salsa club with Cuban food, rum cocktails and great dance music. Go late. *Carrer de Curniola 23. Open Fri–Sun 2000–0400.*

Pla de Sant Joan ⓭ The open space behind the harbour is the setting for several late-night clubs and bars, mostly based in old warehouses. The best include Lateral discotheque and bars Costa Este, Es Giog and Wee Kee Lee.

Opposite: Ciutadella harbour

TIPPING

Restaurant bills include a service charge but it is usual to leave an extra tip of around 5–10 per cent for good service. In bars you usually pay for all drinks when you leave and the custom is to leave your small change behind.

Food and drink

Restaurants in Menorca cater for a wide range of tastes – in the larger resorts you can get anything from an English breakfast to a Chinese take-away. Traditional Menorcan cuisine, however, is typically Mediterranean, making full use of local products – especially seafood – and heavily flavoured with garlic, tomatoes and herbs.

FISH AND SEAFOOD

Local fish and seafood are always excellent – prawns and mussels feature on almost every menu, and squid, swordfish and sole are all widely available. Fish is sometimes baked in the oven with potatoes, tomatoes and breadcrumbs, but you can usually ask for it to be simply grilled. The most famous seafood dish of all is *caldereta de langosta*, a lobster casserole served in an earthenware bowl. You can eat this all over the island, but the best place is definitely beside the harbour at Fornells (*see page 77*).

MEATS

The Menorcans are also hearty meat-eaters. Charcoal grills are a speciality, as are roast suckling pig and shoulder of lamb. Every bar has its own *jamón serrano*, a whole cured ham which is sliced into sandwiches or nibbled with pre-dinner drinks. The local *sobrasada* sausage, made by mincing raw pork with hot peppers, is delicious on toast.

PAELLA

The classic Spanish dish is *paella*, a mound of steaming rice flavoured with saffron and topped with everything from mussels and prawns to pieces of chicken. *Paella* is available everywhere in Menorca, but be wary of anyone who says they can serve you *paella* immediately – if cooked properly it takes at least 20 minutes to produce.

PIZZA

Pizza may not be a local dish, but the pizzas on Menorca are some of the best you will find anywhere. Most pizzerias cook them the Italian way, in a traditional wood-fired oven, with a thin, crisp base and toppings ranging from grilled vegetables to Mahón cheese.

TAPAS

These Spanish snacks are designed to whet the appetite before a meal, but order several portions and it can make an interesting meal in itself. They are usually lined up beneath the bar in metal trays, so it is easy to pick out what you want and point to it. Typical *tapas* include tripe with onions, fried squid rings and meatballs in tomato sauce, but two of the best and simplest are *tortilla*, a cold potato omelette, and *pa amb oli*, toast rubbed with tomato and garlic and sprinkled with olive oil.

DESSERTS

Most restaurants offer a choice of fresh fruit or ice-cream – La Menorquina ice-creams, which originated in Alaior, are popular throughout Spain. An unusual local dessert is *crema catalana*, a custard with a caramelised sugar topping. If you don't have a sweet tooth, you can always ask for a plate of Mahón cheese, a strongly flavoured, hard cheese produced in Alaior (*see page 83*).

WINE AND BEER

The best Spanish wines come from Rioja, though reds and whites from the Penedés region are often better value and Cava, or Spanish champagne, makes an inexpensive and special treat. Beer (*cerveza*) is usually lager, sold either bottled or draught – if you want draught, ask for *una caña*. Bars in the resorts have a wide selection of imported beers from Britain, Germany and elsewhere.

Other alcoholic drinks

Gin has been produced on Menorca for hundreds of years and the best comes from the Xoriguer distillery in Maó. You can drink it neat or with tonic, but the classic Menorcan drink, always drunk at festivals, is *pomada*, or gin with lemon. Most bars have a good array of Spanish brandies on display. *Sangría* is an alcoholic fruit punch based on brandy, red wine and lemonade – delicious, but much more potent than it tastes. Try sangria made with champagne.

Soft drinks

The tap water is safe to drink but most people prefer mineral water – *agua con gas* is sparkling, *agua sin gas* is still. Popular drinks, such as Coca Cola and lemonade, are available everywhere, and some bars offer freshly squeezed fruit juice or *granizado*, a fruit drink with crushed ice. The Spanish always ask for *café solo* after dinner – a small shot of strong, dark coffee, like an espresso – but visitors should have no trouble ordering a *café con leche*, made with hot milk, or a *descafeinado*, decaffeinated coffee.

EATING OUT – A FEW TIPS

- The Spanish tend to eat very late. In the larger resorts it should be possible to get a meal at any time of day, but in Maó, Ciutadella and the inland towns most restaurants do not open before 1300 for lunch and 2000 for dinner – and most people come a lot later than this.

- Many restaurants offer a *menú del día* at lunchtime, a set, three-course meal, including wine or water, at a very good price. There is not usually much choice but the food is always filling, local and fresh.

- Don't be afraid to try local restaurants – most have English menus and even if not the waiter will usually be able to explain what's on the menu.

Menu decoder

aceitunas aliñadas — marinated olives

albóndigas en salsa — meatballs in (usually tomato) sauce

albóndigas de pescado — fish cakes

allioli — garlic-flavoured mayonnaise served as an accompaniment to just about anything – a rice dish, vegetables, shellfish – or as a dip for bread

bistek or *biftek* — beef steak; rare is *poco hecho*, *regular* is medium and *muy hecho* is well done

bocadillo — the Spanish sandwich, usually made of French-style bread

caldereta — a stew based on fish or lamb

caldo — a soup or broth

carne — meat; *carne de ternera* is beef; *carne picada* is minced meat; *carne de cerdo* is pork; *carne de cordero* is lamb

chorizo — a cured, dry red-coloured sausage made from chopped pork, paprika, spices, herbs and garlic

churros — flour fritters cooked in spiral shapes in very hot fat and cut into strips, best dunked into hot chocolate

cordero asado — roast lamb flavoured with lemon and white wine

embutidos charcuteria — pork meat preparations including *jamón* (ham), *chorizo* (see above), *salchichones* (sausages) and *morcillas* (black pudding)

ensalada — salad; the normal restaurant salad is composed of lettuce, onion, tomato and olives

ensalada mixta — as above, but with extra ingredients, such as boiled egg, tuna fish or asparagus

escabeche — a sauce of fish, meat or vegetables cooked in wine and vinegar and left to go cold

estofado de buey — beef stew, made with carrots and turnips, or with potatoes

fiambre — any type of cold meat such as ham, *chorizo*, etc

flan — caramel custard, the national dessert of Spain

fritura — a fry up, as in *fritura de pescado* – different kinds of fried fish

gambas — prawns; *gambas a la plancha* are grilled, *gambas al ajillo* are fried with garlic and *gambas con gabardina* deep fried in batter

gazpacho andaluz — cold soup (originally from Andalucía) made from tomatoes, cucumbers, peppers, bread, garlic and olive oil *gazpacho manchego* (not to be confused with *gazpacho andaluz*) a hot dish made with meat (chicken or rabbit) and unleavened bread

habas con jamón broad beans fried with diced ham (sometimes with chopped hard boiled egg and parsley)

helado ice-cream

jamón ham; *jamón serrano* and *jamón iberico* (far more expensive) are dry cured; cooked ham is *jamón de york*

langostinos a la plancha large prawns grilled and served with vinaigrette or *allioli*; *langostinos a la marinera* are cooked in white wine

lenguado sole, often served cooked with wine and mushrooms

mariscos shellfish

menestra a dish of mixed vegetables cooked separately and combined before serving

menú del día set menu for the day at a fixed price; it may or may not include bread, wine and a dessert, but it doesn't usually include coffee

paella famous rice dish originally from Valencia but now made all over Spain; *paella valenciana* has chicken and rabbit; *paella de mariscos* is made with seafood; *paella mixta* combines meat and seafood

pan bread; *pan de molde* is sliced white bread; wholemeal bread is *pan integral*

pincho moruno pork kebab: spicy chunks of pork on a skewer

pisto the Spanish version of ratatouille, made with tomato, peppers, onions, garlic, courgette and aubergines

pollo al ajillo chicken fried with garlic; *pollo a la cerveza* is cooked in beer; *pollo al chilindrón* is cooked with peppers, tomatoes and onions

salpicón de mariscos seafood salad

sopa de ajo delicious warming winter garlic soup thickened with bread, usually with a poached egg floating in it

tarta helada a popular ice-cream cake served as dessert

ternasco asado roast lamb flavoured with lemon and white wine

tortilla de patatas the classic omelette, also called *tortilla española*, made with potatoes; it can be eaten hot or cold; if you want a plain omelette (with nothing in it) ask for a *tortilla francesa*

zarzuela de pescado y mariscos a stew made with white fish and shellfish in a tomato, wine and saffron stock

Shopping

Every resort has at least one souvenir shop, but for the widest choice of local crafts you should wander around the old towns of Maó and Ciutadella or visit some of the factory shops strung out along the main road between the two. Es Plans, just outside Alaior, has a good selection of leather goods, pottery and jewellery, while Castillo Menorca, in a mock castle near Ferreries, has a Lladró porcelain shop as well as shoes, handbags, Mallorca pearls and lace. Llonga, in the industrial estate outside Ciutadella, has a wide choice of costume jewellery and leather goods.

Another good place for picking up bargains is at the weekly outdoor general markets which tour the island's main towns. The best are in the Plaça de S'Esplanada in Maó (*Tues & Sat mornings*) and the Plaça d'es Born in Ciutadella (*Fri & Sat mornings*). On Saturday mornings there is a craft and produce market in Ferreries. Other markets can be found at Es Castell (*Mon & Wed*), Sant Lluís (*Mon & Wed*), Alaior (*Thurs*), Es Mercadal (*Sun*), Es Migjorn Gran (*Wed*) and fresh produce markets every Mon–Sat morning in Maó and Ciutadella.

SHOES
Menorcan leather is wonderfully soft, and many of the shoes sold with Italian designer labels were actually produced in Menorca. Shop around and you can pick up some real bargains. Anything by Looky, Patricia, Torres, Gomila, Pons Quintana or Jaime Mascaro is likely to be good quality – Jaime Mascaro shoes are sold from a factory shop just outside Ferreries. A Menorcan speciality is *abarcas*, traditional leather sandals made by stitching two pieces of cowhide on to a pneumatic sole. These are so popular that you can even buy pottery versions as souvenirs!

FOOD AND DRINK

Mahón cheese, one of the best in Spain, makes a good souvenir to take home – it is sold in square loaves coated with yellow rind, and comes in several varieties, from young to very mature. Other good buys are almond biscuits, Spanish wine and brandy and Xoriguer gin, sold in earthenware bottles called *canecas*.

MAO AIRPORT

Don't worry if you've left your shopping to the last minute – the airport has a good souvenir shop and a well-stocked tax-paid shop selling drinks, perfume and cigarettes. Visitors returning to other countries in the European Union can take unlimited perfume and wine, and any items bought in Menorcan shops – as long as you have kept the receipt to show that you have paid the tax.

Kids

Menorca is the perfect destination for a holiday with children. The locals adore children and will make a fuss of them wherever you go – even in the smartest restaurants. There are lots of child-friendly beaches, with safe, shallow water, Red Cross posts, beach toys and ice-creams for sale, and pedalos for hire. Most of the resorts have adventure playgrounds, sometimes with toboggan slopes and water-slides, and there are plenty of kids' clubs where your children can be looked after during the day while you relax without them. Your holiday representative will be able to give you information about these.

Children love anything that moves. A boat tour around Maó harbour (*see page 30*) or a cruise along the south coast from Cala Galdana (*see page 58*) can become a real adventure with children on board. The same goes for a tour of one of the larger resorts on a mini-train – you can find these at Punta Prima, Cala'n Porter, Son Bou, Cala Caldana, Cala'n Bosch and Cala'n Bruch.

Pony rides are available in Sant Tomàs (*see page 53*) or at Picadero Menorca, just outside Alaior on the road to Son Bou (*tel: 971 371852*). Another attraction for kids is the equestrian show held at the Club Escola Menorquina (*tel: 971 373497*) on Wednesday and Sunday evenings. This features carriage rides and displays of horsemanship, and children are taken for a donkey ride in the interval. The club is near Ferreries on the road to Cala Galdana. Also, Espectacle Ecuestre, 1 km further on, has shows on Tuesdays and Thursdays.

Menorca's top children's attraction is probably the Club San Jaime at Son Bou. With a swimming pool, a water-slide and an interlocking maze, there is enough here to keep children happy for hours (*see page 49*).

Sports and activities

Menorca is the perfect place for a relaxing holiday and for many people the most exercise they get is a walk to the beach followed by a quick swim in the sea – but if it's an active holiday you are after there are plenty of opportunities. The calm, clear waters of Menorca's sheltered coves make excellent conditions for watersports, while the gentle countryside inland is ideal for walking, cycling and horse riding.

WATERSPORTS

Sailing and windsurfing schools include, Surf'n'Sail Menorca at Son Xoriguer (*tel: 971 387090*), Windsurf Fornells at the entrance to Fornells (*tel: 971 376400*), and Sports Massanet in Ciutadella harbour (*tel: 971 482186*). All of them offer tuition to beginners and can also hire out equipment. The clear waters around Menorca's coves are ideal for snorkelling, but if you want to see more of the marine life, and get inside some of the caves, you could try scuba diving. Courses for beginners and more advanced divers are offered at Ulmo in Addaia (*tel: 971 188996*), Hotel Poseidon at Cala Santandría (*tel: 971 382644*), Cala Torret near Binibeca (*tel: 971 188530*), the Diving Centre in Fornells (*tel: 971 376431*) and S'Algar Diving and Aquasports (*tel: 971 150601; e-mail: enquiry@salgardiving.com; http://www.salgardiving.com*). Crystal Seas Scuba in Cala'n Bosch marina also runs diving courses as well as deep-sea fishing trips. Remember that it is dangerous to fly within 24 hours of diving.

HORSE RIDING

Pony and horse hire, and riding lessons, are available from the following centres:

- Picadero Binixica, on the main road through Sant Climent. *Tel: 971 153071.*
- Picadero Menorca, on the road from Alaior to Son Bou. *Tel: 971 371852.*
- Equimar, off the Maó to Es Castell road. *Tel: 971 369112.*

● Es Boeret, at S'Algar near
   Sant Lluís. *Tel: 971 151049.*

WALKING AND CYCLING

Menorca Velo and Menorca
Trekking, branches of Club Activ
(*tel: 971 373843*) organise a
range of day excursions into
Menorca's hidden countryside –
these can usually be booked in
your resort. Bike hire is also
available in the larger resorts for
those who want to head off on
their own. There are lots of lovely
walks around the coastline, to
secret coves that cannot be
reached by road – two of the best
and easiest walks are from Cala
Galdana to Cala Macarella and
Son Parc to Cala Pudent.

OTHER SPORTING ACTIVITIES

● Cricket – join the MCC (Menorca Cricket Club) for a game on the only
   grass pitch in Spain, at Biniparrell near Sant Lluís. *Tel: 971 150807.*
● Golf – the nine-hole course at Son Parc (*page 79*) is open to visitors.
   Tel: 971 188875.
● Karting – beside the hippodrome on the Maó to Sant Lluís road or at
   Castillo Menorca, on the main road from Ferreries to Ciutadella. Both
   are open all day.
● Snooker – there are two full-size tables at Scandals restaurant in Es
   Castell. *Open 1100–2300. Tel: 971 365313.*
● Tennis – there are courts in the larger resorts and also in Maó.

Festivals and events

MUSIC AND FOLK DANCING

A lively display of local music and dancing is usually on offer at weekends in main towns and resorts. Times and places are advertised in bars around the main squares of each town or in the local press.

JAZZ

The only place to hear live jazz is at Casino San Clemente, on the main street of Sant Climent, from 2130 on Tuesdays and Thursdays (*see page 38*). Visiting musicians are welcome to join in. Asere, in Carrer Corniola, is a lively late-night salsa club.

CONCERTS

Classical music lovers should look out for the international festivals held in Maó and Ciutadella in July and August – details of concerts can be found in local papers or on posters in the cities. There are also daily morning organ concerts from Monday to Saturday in the church of Santa Maria in Maó.

FESTIVALS

Every town in Menorca has its annual festival, in honour of its patron saint, with street parties, fireworks, and displays of horse riding in the main square. Some of the largest festivals take place in Es Castell (24–26 July), Ferreries (23–25 August) and Maó (7–9 September), but the biggest and most colourful of all is the festival of Sant Joan (St John), held in Ciutadella on 23–25 June. It begins with a horseback procession and ends with a massive firework display in Plaça d'es Born – and in between are two days of riotous festivities, all fuelled by large amounts of *pomada*, or gin with lemon.

HORSES

The Menorcan passion for horses can also be seen at the trotting races which take place each weekend at the racetracks outside Maó and Ciutadella. The jockey sits in a small cart behind the horse and his job is to make it go as fast as possible without breaking into a gallop. There is a fun family atmosphere and most people have a small bet on the horses. The races begin at around 1800 in Maó on Saturdays and Ciutadella at 1800 on Sundays.

Club Escola Menorquina, on the road from Ferreries to Cala Galdana, gives twice-weekly demonstrations of typically Menorcan dressage skills at their riding stables. During the interval, there are donkey rides for the children.

Taking better holiday photos

All professional photographers know that it's not the camera that takes good pictures, it's the photographer. David Bailey takes stunning pictures using a cheap throwaway camera, and we all know the show-offs with the expensive lenses who still cannot take a decent picture. The truth is that camera technology is now so good that anyone can take top-quality pictures, if you follow a few simple rules.

Choose the correct film for the lighting conditions: film stock is available in different speeds depending on the lighting conditions. Fast film – 100 ASA – is best for the bright light you will experience at most resorts, where the brightness of the sun is enhanced by reflections from the sand and water. Slow film – 400 ASA – is better for indoor photography or anywhere that you would need to use flash – for architectural shots in shade, for example. If, like most photographers, you want to take a mix of indoor and outdoor pictures, buy an intermediate speed of film – 200 ASA is ideal.

Use light to your advantage: everybody knows the golden rule that you should never take a picture directly into the sun – ideally the sun should be behind you, so that the light falls where you want it – on the subject of your photograph. But all rules can be broken to advantage: shooting into the sun can be used to create a back-lit effect, whereby the sun creates a silhouette around the subject – even more effective at sunset.

Use shadows: the opposite of sunlight is shadow, and many professional photographers prefer to take pictures early in the day, when the sun is low and the shadows are deep, rather than during the main part of the day, when every detail is equally lit. Shadows enhance the details of sculpture and architecture: even a boring wall can become an interesting subject if shadows enhance the texture.

Avoid the harsh light of the hottest part of the day: another reason for avoiding harsh sunlight is that it has the effect of bleaching colour; that is why the blue sky looks white on your photographs, and why intensely coloured flowers look pale and washed out. The best time for photography is early in the morning and later in the afternoon, in the soft magical hours before dusk. If you do take photos during the day, wait for the sun to go behind a cloud, which helps to diffuse and soften the harsh light.

Get up close to your subject: the big mistake that every amateur photographer makes is to try and cram too much into the picture. Good photographs are ones that choose a detail that stands for the whole. Take a picture of a stone sculpture, rather than the whole of the church façade; of a single orchid rather than the whole of the flower-filled meadow; of a water-filled rockpool rather than the whole sweep of beach.

Catch the family unawares: try to avoid the obvious pose when taking pictures of your friends and family. Better still, try to avoid posing them at all – candid photographs (those that are taken without the subject being aware) are often far better than posed ones, because the subject is relaxed and looks more like their normal selves, rather than wearing an artificial smile or a cheesy grin. Take pictures of your family as they eat, shop and fool around – bringing life and movement into the photograph.

Tell a story: ask yourself, as you compose the picture, what is this picture about and will it interest another person? Think like a photo journalist as you look for picture subjects that will arouse curiosity and make the viewer want to take a second look. You want people to say, as they look at your pictures, 'that is interesting', not 'what a bore!'.

And finally … use a reputable film-processing company. Don't trust your precious holiday pictures to any old express film-processing service, or the investment you have made in good-quality film stock and careful composition will be thrown away. If in doubt, wait until you get home before having your pictures developed, and use a processor whose standards you know and trust.

Getting to Menorca

The cheapest way to get to Menorca is to book a package holiday with one of the leading tour operators, such as Thomas Cook or JMC. Tour operators specialising in Menorca offer flight-only deals or combined flight-and-accommodation

packages at prices that are hard to beat by booking direct. If your travelling times are flexible, and if you can avoid the school holidays, you can also find some very cheap last-minute deals using websites such as www.thomascook.com.

BY AIR

The majority of visitors use charter companies to get to Menorca, which operate from nearly all of the UK's regional airports. Menorca's modern airport is also served by scheduled international flights from the UK and by internal flights from Spanish airports at Madrid, Valencia and Barcelona. Flights are offered by the Spanish national carrier, Iberia Airlines, and by British Airways. Iberia's UK office is at Venture House, 27–29 Glasshouse Street, London W1R 6JU, tel: 020 7830 0011; fax: 020 7413 1261. British Airways can be contacted on 0845 773 3377 (fares, availability, and bookings); or at any of their Travel Shops (tel: 0845 606 0747); or via their website at: www.britishairways.com.

SPANISH TOURIST OFFICE

Further information about the Menorca can be obtained from the Spanish National Tourist Office, 22-23 Manchester Square, London W1M 5AP, tel: 020 7486 8077; fax: 020 7486 8034. It is best to write or visit in person as the telephone lines are heavily used, or you can consult the Spanish National Tourist Office web site at: www.tourspain.es.

First-time traveller's guide

BEFORE YOU GO

Holidays should be about fun and relaxation, so avoid last-minute panics and stress by making your preparations well in advance.

Passports: Make sure that your passports are up to date and have at least three months left to run (to be safe, six months is even better). All children (new-born babies upwards) need their own passport now, unless they are already included on the passport of the person they are travelling with – in which case they can continue to travel abroad with the passport holder until they reach the age of 16. Remember that it takes at least three weeks to renew or obtain a passport. Ring the Passport Agency on 0990 210410, or access its website (www.ukpa.gov.uk), for details of the current passport processing times, and how to apply for a passport or renew an existing one.

Money: You will need some currency before you go, especially if your flight gets you to your destination at the weekend or late in the day after the banks have closed. Traveller's cheques are the safest way to carry money because the money will be refunded if the cheques are lost or stolen. To buy traveller's cheques or exchange money at a bank you may need to give up to a week's notice, depending on the quantity of foreign currency you require. You can exchange money at the airport before you depart. You should also make sure that your credit, charge and debit cards are up to date – you do not want them to expire mid holiday – and that your credit limit is sufficient to allow you to make those holiday purchases. Don't forget, too, to check your PIN numbers in case you haven't used them for a while – you may want to draw money from cash dispensers while you are away. Ring your bank or card company and they will help you out.

INSURANCE

Have you got sufficient cover for your holiday? Check that your policy covers you adequately for loss of possessions and valuables, for activities you might want to try – such as scuba-diving, horse-riding, or watersports – and for emergency medical and dental treatment, including flights home if required.

HEALTH MATTERS

You do not need inoculations to travel within Europe, but it is worth checking that you and your family are up to date with the basics, such as tetanus. If you take prescription medicines, make sure you have enough to last the whole trip. Consider packing a small first-aid kit containing plasters, antiseptic cream, travel sickness pills, insect repellent and/or bite-relief cream, upset stomach remedies, painkillers and sun lotions.

PETS

Remember to make arrangements for the care of your pets while you are away – book them into a reputable cat or dog hotel, or make arrangements with a trustworthy neighbour to ensure that they are properly fed, watered and exercised while you are on holiday.

SECURITY

Take sensible precautions to prevent your house being burgled while you are away:

- Cancel milk, newspapers and other regular deliveries so that post and milk does not pile up on the doorstep, indicating that you are away.
- Let the postman know where to leave parcels and bulky mail that will not go through your letterbox – ideally with a next-door neighbour.
- If possible, arrange for a friend or neighbour to visit regularly, closing and opening curtains in the evening and morning, and switching lights on and off to give the impression that the house is being lived in.
- Consider buying electrical timing devices that will switch lights and radios on and off, again to give the impression that there is someone in the house.
- Let Neighbourhood Watch representatives and the police know that you will be away so that they can keep an eye on your home.
- If you have a burglar alarm, make sure that it is serviced and working properly and is switched on when you leave (you may find that your insurance policy requires this). Ensure that a neighbour is able to gain access to the alarm to turn it off if it is set off accidentally.
- If you are leaving cars unattended, put them in a garage, if possible, and leave a key with a neighbour in case the alarm goes off.

AIRPORT PARKING AND ACCOMMODATION

If you intend to leave your car in an airport car park while you are away, or stay the night at an airport hotel before or after your flight, you should book well ahead to take advantage of discounts or cheap off-airport parking. Airport accommodation gets booked up several weeks in advance, especially during the height of the holiday season. Check whether the hotel offers free parking for the duration of the holiday – often the savings made on parking costs can significantly reduce the accommodation price.

PACKING TIPS

Baggage allowances vary according to the airline, destination and the class of travel, but 20 kilos per person is the norm for luggage that is carried in the hold (it usually tells you what the weight limit is on your ticket). You are also allowed one item of cabin baggage weighing no more than 5 kilos, and measuring 46 by 30 by 23 cm (18 by 12 by 9 inches). In addition, you can usually carry your duty-free purchases, umbrella, handbag, coat, camera, etc, as hand baggage. Large items – surfboards, golf-clubs, collapsible wheelchairs and pushchairs – are usually charged as extras and it is a good idea to let the airline know in advance that you want to bring these.

CHECK-IN, PASSPORT CONTROL AND CUSTOMS

First-time travellers can often find airport security intimidating, but it is all very easy really.

- Check-in desks usually open two or three hours before the flight is due to depart. Arrive early for the best choice of seats.

- Look for your flight number on the TV monitors in the check-in area, and find the relevant check-in desk. Your tickets will be checked and your luggage taken. Take your boarding card and go to the departure gate. Here your hand luggage will be X-rayed and your passport checked.

- In the departure area, you can shop and relax, but watch the monitors that tell you when to board – usually about 30 minutes before take-off. Go to the departure gate shown on the monitor and follow the instructions given to you by the airline staff.

Editorial and production

Project Management: Dial House Publishing

Managing Editor for Thomas Cook Publishing: Deborah Parker

Design: Wenham Arts

Editing and proofreading: Dial House Publishing

Picture research: Michelle Warrington

Map Editor for Thomas Cook Publishing: Bernard Horton

Maps redrawn by: Polly Senior Cartography

2002 Edition

Project Management: Cambridge Publishing Management Ltd

Layout and repro: Cambridge Publishing Management Ltd

Printed and bound by: Artes Gráficas Elkar, Loiu, Spain

Acknowledgements

We would like to thank all the photographers, picture libraries and organisations for the loan of the photographs reproduced in this book, to whom copyright in the photograph belongs:

Chris Fairclough (pages 3 and 40);

Teresa Fisher (pages 6, 9, 15, 23, 24, 32, 66, 85, 86, 88, 95 and 124);

JMC (pages 16, 35, 46, 52 and 102);

J Allan Cash (pages 48, 62, 90 and 106);

Spectrum (pages 39, 60, 72, 74, 78, 97, 101, 105, 113, 114, 120 and 123);

Image Select (page 117);

Spanish National Tourist Board (page 119);

Foto Dolfo, Maó (page 26).